"A generation ago, capitalism's supposed triumph was seen by many as unassailable. But several years of soaring inequality, the looming threat of ecological disaster, and the erosion of even the pretence of democracy in the political process, have led millions of people, especially young people, to lose confidence in the system. As these young workers and students seek out a concise yet comprehensive account of why capitalism is failing them, and a compelling sketch of some feasible and attractive alternatives to it, they will find no better starting point than Tom Malleson's lucid and intelligent book, *Fired Up about Capitalism.*"

> — STEPHEN D'ARCY, Associate Professor of
> Philosophy, Huron University College, and author
> of *Languages of the Unheard: Why Militant Protest
> is Good for Democracy*

"Tom Malleson's *Fired Up about Capitalism* is a rare and wonderful book. It is wonderful because it provides such a compelling analysis of some of the most pressing economic and political problems of our time along with both short-term and long-term solutions. It is rare because it is written in a way that is rigorous, sophisticated, and nuanced while at the same time being clear, engaging, and accessible, without jargon or pretension. *Fired Up about Capitalism* should be widely read both by seasoned activists wanting to sharpen their critique of capitalism and their understanding of alternatives, and by interested readers with little background in these issues."

— ERIK OLIN WRIGHT, Professor of Sociology, University of Wisconsin, author of *Envisioning Real Utopias*

"Tom Malleson's timely book *Fired Up about Capitalism* provides a clear and inspirational outline to the problems of our collective world's social, political, and economic crises, as well as some thoughtful arguments for their immediate and long-term resolution. This book presents complex issues with honesty, passion, and scholarship and is filled with that all too rare element of hope. It is well placed to be an inspiration to a generation of activists and students."

— J.J. MCMURTRY, Associate Professor, Business and Society Program, York University

"Tom Malleson's *Fired Up about Capitalism* is an amazing accomplishment: an incisive yet accessible critique of contemporary capitalist society, and a set of clear ideas about how we can collectively do better. Malleson's arguments are motivated by strong moral reasoning, but always supported by careful empirical evidence. This is an exciting and important book, and one that will surely motivate a new generation of activists."

— DAVID WACHSMUTH, Assistant Professor of Urban Planning, McGill University

"In clear and concise terms, *Fired Up about Capitalism* offers an agenda for activists to adopt. Such books are sorely needed to spur on the kind of dialogue that, through agreement and disagreement, can help us forge a collective path forward."

— UMAIR MUHAMMAD, author of *Confronting Injustice: Social Activism in the Age of Individualism*

"Malleson is a public intellectual of the first rate, brilliantly combining scholarly acumen with activist passion and know-how. In *Fired Up about Capitalism* he offers a frontal assault on the demoralizing notion that "There is No Alternative to Capitalism" (TINA). This short book is not merely a critique of the inequality, hierarchy, greed, injustice, and environmental devastation wrought by neoliberal capitalism. It is also an invigorating defense of radical democracy and a welcome wake-up call about real alternatives that already exist."

— CRAIG BOROWIAK, author of *Accountability and Democracy: the Pitfalls and Promise of Popular Control* and Associate Professor of Political Science, Haverford College

"Tom Malleson is fired up *against* capitalism—his powerful indictment backed by a plethora of well-chosen data. He defends, not only social-democratic reforms, but more radical (and more controversial) long-term institutional changes that would take us *beyond* capitalism. With so many people in so many countries becoming ever more aware that the current "system" isn't working, this beautifully written book could scarcely be more timely."

— DAVID SCHWEICKART, Professor of Philosophy, Loyola University Chicago

"Tom Malleson once again has hit the critical mark. In clear and crisp language, Malleson pithily summarizes what is wrong with neoliberal capitalism while presenting a compelling case for the many alternatives to it that are within our reach. Shifting from the social, economic, and environmental injustices and inequalities wrought by the status quo and its mantra of "there is no alternative," to myriad achievable proposals that can proliferate into a different socio-economic reality, it's all here in a 21st century manifesto of radical democracy from one of Canada's most insightful activist-academics."

— MARCELO VIETA, Assistant Professor in the Program in Adult Education and Community Development, Ontario Institute for Studies in Education of the University of Toronto

FIRED UP ABOUT
CAPITALISM

TOM MALLESON

Between the Lines
Toronto

First published in 2016 by Between the Lines
401 Richmond Street West
Studio 277
Toronto, Ontario M5V 3A8
Canada
1-800-718-7201
www.btlbooks.com

Library and Archives Canada Cataloguing in Publication

Malleson, Tom, author
Fired up about capitalism / Tom Malleson.
(Fired up books)

Includes index.
Issued in print and electronic formats.

ISBN 978-1-77113-200-8 (paperback).—ISBN 978-1-77113-201-5 (epub).—
ISBN 978-1-77113-202-2 (pdf)

1. Capitalism—Moral and ethical aspects.   2. Capitalism—Social aspects.   I. Title.

HB501.M287 2016   330.12'2   C2016-901829-6
C2016-901830-X

Cover design by Jennifer Tiberio
Cover illustration by Jack Dylan
Text design by Gordon Robertson
Printed in Canada

RECYCLED
Paper made from
recycled material
FSC
www.fsc.org   FSC® C103567

GCC/IBT

We acknowledge for their financial support of our publishing activities the Government of Canada through the Canada Book Fund, the Canada Council for the Arts, which last year invested $153 million to bring the arts to Canadians throughout the country, and the Government of Ontario through the Ontario Arts Council, the Ontario Book Publishers Tax Credit program, and the Ontario Media Development Corporation.

  Canada Council   Conseil des Arts
for the Arts   du Canada

 Canadä

ONTARIO ARTS COUNCIL
CONSEIL DES ARTS DE L'ONTARIO
an Ontario government agency
un organisme du gouvernement de l'Ontario

This book is dedicated to Lesley Wood, Mac Scott, and David McNally—my role models in showing me that growing up need not mean outgrowing activism.

A map of the world that does not include Utopia is not worth even glancing at, for it leaves out the one country at which Humanity is always landing. And when Humanity lands there, it looks out, and, seeing a better country, sets sail. Progress is the realisation of Utopias.

— OSCAR WILDE,
"The Soul of Man under Socialism"

CONTENTS

ACKNOWLEDGEMENTS

Everything I write is written with the thoughts of others' minds. This project, like all activist endeavours, has been a collaborative one.

Many deep thanks to Daniel Cohen, Rebecca Hall, David Lizoain, Roey Malleson (without whom literally nothing would be possible), Sarah Mikhaiel, Seth Prins, David Wachsmuth, and the two anonymous reviewers. In particular I owe Laura Burns a debt of gratitude for her unwavering support.

Thanks to my diligent editor, Amanda Crocker, and the whole Between the Lines team. I am also grateful to Tilman Lewis for his meticulous copy editing.

Most importantly I would like to thank the countless activists and organizers whose struggle and dedication inspire every page. The things I know, they have taught me. The mistakes I reserve for myself.

INTRODUCTION

I N 1962 the influential right-wing economist Milton Friedman famously declared that there were only two real possibilities for modern complex societies. They could be a free market system (like the United States), or a centrally planned system (like the Soviet Union).[1] Twenty years later, British prime minister Margaret Thatcher went one step further. She declared that since the Russian system was morally and economically bankrupt, there was no alternative at all to free market capitalism. She summed up this thought with the slogan: *there is no alternative* (TINA).

Today TINA is the prevailing philosophy of the richest and most powerful people in the world. Politicians declare it daily, journalists parrot it, and talk show hosts acquiesce to it. Rich people gloat about TINA and regular people simply assume it. The rich and powerful have many weapons—their billions of dollars, their bought-and-paid-for politicians, their media empires, even their military might. But none may be as powerful in securing the capitalist system as the ability to convince regular people that there simply is no alternative.

TINA is the ultimate ideological shield. It is the most powerful defence of capitalism because it can deflect any kind of criticism whatsoever. Is it really necessary for chief executive officers (CEOs) to make two hundred times more than average workers?[2] TINA. How is it just for the giant pharmaceutical company Pfizer to develop no new drugs for tuberculosis (which kills about two million poor people a year in Africa), but instead develop in one single year eight new drugs for impotence and seven new drugs for balding to sell to wealthy Americans?[3] TINA. Shouldn't we be worried that greenhouse gas emissions from our planes and factories are making the ice caps melt faster than at any time in recorded history? TINA. Does software magnate Bill Gates really need $40 billion[4] while 48 million of his neighbouring citizens have to go to foodbanks? TINA!

MY POLITICAL AWAKENING

As a teenager, I remember sitting beside my grandpa in the English countryside as he told stories of his life in South Africa. His family had fled the anti-Jewish pogroms in Russia in the early 1900s. They ended up in Johannesburg, where he grew up.

He spent most of his life in South Africa fighting against apartheid—the country's infamous system of racial segregation—as a member of the Communist party. He was convinced that capitalism was a fundamentally rotten system and that sooner or later it would fall apart and be replaced with communism. So I would sit on his porch watching the sunset and listening to his stories of the African National Congress, and its leader, Nelson Mandela, in jail for twenty-seven years before becoming the country's first black president. Grandpa spoke of the terrible curse of racism, of capitalist greed and of communist hope.

He had many stories to tell of his apartheid-fighting days. You used to have to sign a formal register for the authorities, he explained, if you wanted to take out a book by Karl Marx from the library. After the Suppression of Communism Act of 1950, progressives were arrested in the dead of the night and kept without charge in dark jail cells where terrible things would happen.

He once received a letter from the government, very formal and polite. It called him "Dear Sir" (since whites had some basic rights), and continued in the most proper, respectful tones to inform him that, as a known communist, they were truly sorry but he was legally liable to be arrested (and presumably tortured) at any time. Thank you for your time and sincerely yours, your faithful servant. . . . Only apartheid-era South Africa could combine British politeness with ominous fascism in a single letter.

I remember feeling proud that Grandpa had been on the right side in South Africa, the side of Mandela and the side of justice. I felt proud that he hadn't let himself be carried along with the current of normalcy, but had stood up to his white community, conservative neighbours, and racist family members. He had risked their disapproval and suffered their scorn because he knew right from wrong. I was proud that Grandpa had called for full and complete equality for black South Africans a good forty years before respectable liberals began to acknowledge that there could be something even a tiny bit unjust about apartheid.

Grandpa was not just hopeful about South Africa. He was hopeful about the world. He was a firm believer that, although capitalism was dominant, there *was* an alternative—it was called the Soviet Union. Yet as time passed, his dream of a socialist utopia appeared more and more remote from the reality of Russia. Facts began coming to light about life in the Soviet states. The show trials where prisoners confessed to crimes they did not commit, and the gulags in Siberia where prisoners were sent to work and die. The crushing of democratic movements in Hungary in the 1950s and Czechoslovakia in the 1960s. The imperialist invasion of Afghanistan in the 1970s. Slowly, my grandpa's faith in the communist alternative crumbled to dust.

The Berlin Wall—which enforced the border of Communist East Germany—came down in 1989, and the Soviet Union collapsed a couple of years later. Capitalists the world over popped champagne corks and joyfully cheered that "history is over!"

The collapse of the Soviet Union demoralized the left. Many communists, like my grandfather, felt that that the Soviet Union had betrayed their hopes. Other lefties who were not communist still shared broad aspirations about the possibility and desirability of transcending capitalism. With the fall of the Wall the world shrank. Political possibilities seemed to narrow. Much of the left gave up on the belief that systemic alternatives to capitalism were possible. Many suffered the bitter thought that perhaps Margaret Thatcher was right after all. Maybe there really was no alternative.

Although I grew up feeling inspired by Grandpa's fight against apartheid, I could never really understand his sadness about the Soviet Union. For my generation, the Soviet Union had never represented anything particularly hopeful, and so its passing was not upsetting.

I was born in the early 1980s and grew up in Vancouver, ensconced in the political amnesia that is Canadian middle-class life. By the time I was a teen in the 1990s and starting to become able to think for myself, I wasn't particularly interested in doing so. I had Tupac tapes to burn and Nike shoes to buy. I had parties to go to, friends to impress, booze to bootleg, and schoolwork to avoid. We had a picture of Mandela on our fridge, but politics seemed far, far away. It seemed something that boring, staid politicians rambled on about, something old-fashioned that happened in countries on the other side of the world. Politics, like Mandela's picture, was something to be glanced at as you opened the fridge looking for something to eat.

But my blissful ignorance couldn't last forever. Everything changed in 1999 when the protests against the World Trade Organization (WTO)—the so-called Battle of Seattle—exploded just three hours down the highway from my house. I was glued to the TV, watching thousands of protesters dancing in the streets, locking hands, singing and chanting, and unceremoniously getting the crap kicked out of them by the cops. I saw a line of young protesters, guys and girls in their early twenties, sitting in a line, linking arms, solemn and determined, with bandanas and goggles on their faces to protect them from tear gas. A police officer walked up to them and, one by one, slowly pulled their goggles away from their faces so he could shoot pepper spray directly into their eyes. I remember hearing the protesters scream.

I had no idea at the time what the WTO was, or what these people's beef was. But it was obvious that they had a lot to say. They had arguments and quotes; they referenced books I'd never heard of. They showed graphs and detailed charts mapping everything from environmental degradation to growing wage inequality. They were amazingly passionate, dedicated, and even joyful. What the hell was going on? Hadn't they received the same memo that my grandpa got—signed by Friedman and Thatcher and all the rest—telling them, in no uncertain terms, that *there is no alternative*?

These protesters considered themselves part of the anti-globalization movement. They said they were social justice activists and organizers, and they appeared not to give a damn about the Soviet Union. "Capitalism is the exploitation of man by man," they would jest. "Communism is just the reverse." These folks were happy to wipe their hands of any allegiance to authoritarian communism and start thinking of better alternatives. Instead of living in apathy and hopelessness, they dared to believe that change was possible.

Well, that was the turning point for me. It was the beginning of my life as a radical and an anti-capitalist, anti-authoritarian activist. I would spend much of the next fifteen years at protests, demonstrations, and meetings. I sang and chanted, read radical books, and had endless conversations with other activists. I learned to cook vegan stews to feed hundreds, began unlearning gender assumptions, joined unions, and participated in building social movements. And, unfortunately, I continued to get tear-gassed along the way.

A DEMOCRATIC IDEAL

These days I'm convinced that when conservatives say *there is no alternative*, they are not saying something that *is* true. How could anyone know what the future holds? They are only saying something that they want to be true. When people use the argument of TINA, it says less about the truth of other economic systems than it does about those people actually liking capitalism.

In fact, history shows that there have always been alternatives. There have always been many different kinds of societies. Even today, there are massive differences between, say, the United States, Brazil, Japan, and Sweden. There are even more differences if we include places such as Venezuela or China. The reason some Americans denounce the Swedes as lazy and living off welfare is the same reason that Venezuelans denounce the American system as exploitative and imperialistic: different systems offer real alternatives.

If there really were no alternative, no one would bother commenting on anyone else. No one would bother talking about politics at all. It may well be that none of these systems are ideal. Indeed it's likely that if we look closely, we'll find aspects of each system that we like as well as aspects that we don't. But to look around the world and say TINA is to intentionally ignore the real possibilities that exist.

I've come to believe that my grandpa's basic belief was right. Capitalism as we know it is a rotten system. What exactly does capitalism mean? What separates capitalist economies from those that came before? The most basic answer is that capitalism is an economic system in which the majority of goods and services are produced and distributed via a market system, that is, through buying and selling of private property.

This is fine as a very general definition, but in many ways it's too broad. Market systems can be shaped in a wide range of ways. They can be shaped to benefit the rich (which is usually the case) or regulated to redistribute wealth to the poor. They can offer no job security or lifetime employment guarantees. They can involve private corporations or democratic worker co-operatives. The United States is a market system, but so are France, Bolivia, and Equatorial Guinea. Generalizing about such different systems tends to obscure more than it reveals.

Indeed, even an ideal democratic socialist society, which is the kind of system I'll argue we should aim for, is a market system. Almost no one today thinks that we should get rid of markets altogether. So talking about the market system is far too broad to capture the most important features of our societies. What I'm most interested in is a particular type of capitalism—the type that rules the contemporary world. It is usually referred to as "neoliberal capitalism."

Neoliberal capitalism (sometimes called "free market capitalism" or simply "neoliberalism") is best captured, I think, by three defining characteristics:

- Businesses, banks, consumers, and workers interact through a *market system that is largely unregulated* (or, more precisely, regulated in ways that primarily benefit the wealthy). This means that private profit is the overriding concern.
- There is significant *class inequality.* Some people are free to live off their parents' trust funds, while most people have to sell their labour to get by.
- Businesses and banks are *undemocratic hierarchies.* They have private owners and managers at the top, and workers at the bottom.

These characteristics define neoliberal countries such as Canada, the United States, the United Kingdom, and so on. Certain countries in Europe have gone a significant way in challenging these things, so they are usually referred to as "social democratic" countries.

My primary argument is that neoliberal capitalism is a rotten system. It is unfree and unequal. It is environmentally destructive, globally unfair, and culturally pernicious.

That doesn't mean it's the worst system that has ever been. Compared to earlier feudalism, capitalist societies are much richer and, in certain important respects, freer. The people are no longer legally bound to their class position. Compared to state communism, capitalism tends to keep power at least somewhat decentralized, which has prevented dictatorship. It has also enabled greater freedom of choice, both in terms of occupation and consumption.

So we need to be nuanced and careful in our thinking. It's tempting to declare one system entirely good and another entirely bad. But the real task is to think through, in a realistic way, how we might combine the positive elements of different systems, while retaining as few of the negative aspects as possible.

I'll also argue that there *are* alternatives. Dozens of them. I don't have a blueprint for a perfect society, and you should probably be sceptical of anyone who says they do. But many of us in the global justice movement share core values and have concrete, practical ideas about how to put these values into practice. Furthermore, many inspiring examples of alternative institutions already exist in small pockets in different places around the world. Learning about these examples is a major way of seeing through the mist of TINA.

Although I learned about the ideas in this book through reading and dialogue with many activists, teachers, and intellectuals in Canada and elsewhere, my take on these ideas is my own. So for the sake of transparency, I'll put my personal cards on the table. I think that there *are* alternatives to neoliberal capitalism. They are based on the traditional values of the left: freedom, equality, solidarity. I'll describe many examples of policies and institutions that embody these values. I'll look at equal freedom at work, equal freedom from having to overwork, respect rather than arrogance toward the planet, and solidarity rather than competition with each other.

If you are looking for one core idea—one general principle for rearranging the economy that could replace the old principles of free markets or central planning—I would suggest that the most promising new principle is that of radical democracy. U.S.-style unregulated, winner-take-all casino capitalism leads to billionaires and homeless people. Soviet-style top-down authoritarian

Liberté, égalité, solidarité

Liberté, égalité, fraternité—or *freedom, equality, brother-hood*—was the rallying cry of the French Revolution. Although "fraternité" is nowadays usually replaced with the less sexist "solidarité," these three continue to be foundational values for the left. It is easy to use these words as a simple slogan. The real task, though, is to construct institutions that truly reflect them.

planning features gulags and group-think. What we need is a different kind of system in which *all* the major institutions—the government, the businesses, the banks—work on the principle of democratic equality. People should have a right to democratic accountability in the economic as well as the political decisions that affect their lives. This means not just political democracy, but also economic democracy.

Moreover, the more that this democracy can be direct and participatory (instead of the occasional once-every-four-years vote) the better. The more that people can actively engage with others, face-to-face, over the decisions that affect their lives, the more they will be free and empowered. What would be the result of all this radical democracy? That's not for me to say; it's up to the population to decide for themselves. But I suspect that if people were empowered in these ways, they would choose to arrange the distribution of wealth and opportunity in a far more egalitarian manner than we see today.

The first chapter of this book explores the birth of the myth of TINA. The second and third chapters lay out the central problems with capitalism: inequality, workplace hierarchy, consumerist greed, global injustice, and environmental degradation. Chapter 4 maps out some of the most exciting and promising short-term alternatives that are available right now. Chapter 5 presents a vision of more radical, long-term changes to work toward for a comprehensive alternative to free market capitalism. And Chapter 6 concludes with a call to get off our asses and build the world that we want to see before it's too late.

A WORLD FOR THE CHANGING

Winston Churchill, prime minister of Britain during the Second World War, famously said, "If you're not a socialist when you're twenty, you have no heart. If you're not a conservative when you're forty, you have no head." This was his version of TINA, his way of saying that capitalism is here to stay.

Well, I for one would rather have my heart than his head. Churchill was a right-wing colonialist and white supremacist who thought that the Indian people weren't capable of governing themselves. He dismissed Mahatma Gandhi—who would non-violently lead India to independence from the British Empire—as a "half naked lunatic fakir" who "ought to be laid, bound hand and foot, at the gates of Delhi and then trampled on by an enormous elephant with the new viceroy seated on its back."

Unfortunately for Mr. Churchill, young people today are showing that perhaps it's his head that wasn't on right. The last few years have seen people revolting across the globe, from the Occupy Wall Street protests in New York, to the anti-austerity protests in Spain and Greece, to the grassroots movements propelling new anti-establishment figures like Bernie Sanders and Jeremy Corbyn, to the youth-led Black Lives Matter protests in North America. Young people are changing the world.

If you read this book and start talking about lefty ideas, it won't be long before someone looks down their nose at you and says *there is no alternative* or condescendingly quotes Churchill. But as much as these people may wish otherwise, there are alternatives. Sorry, Churchill, but we have hearts *and* heads. And we're not going away.

1

THE
MYTH
OF
TINA

THESE DAYS, the neoliberal belief that there is no alternative to the free market is so commonplace that it's almost taken for granted. It's easy to think that this consensus has existed forever. In fact, it's surprisingly new.

In the 1970s practically no one was a neoliberal. Only a few decades ago it was widely agreed that free markets could not be left to themselves. The market needed state regulation and wealth needed at least some redistribution. Indeed, the Republican U.S. president Richard Nixon even implemented price controls—limits on what businesses were allowed to charge for certain products. That's about as far from the worship of free markets as you can get. That same decade the Canadian Liberal government called for nationalizing the country's oil. They felt that private corporations couldn't be trusted to ensure cheap, fair access for all Canadians to such a vital resource.

Today the political landscape looks very different. Not even the most radical member of the Democratic Party in the United States, the Labour Party in the United Kingdom, or the New Democratic Party in Canada would dare to advocate for price controls or nationalization. They'd be afraid of being screamed out of office.

How did mainstream political common sense shift so dramatically to the right?

THE BIRTH OF THE MYTH

A good place to start is the year 1944. The Western world was finally emerging, thanks to massive state spending for the Second World War, from the greatest depression that capitalism had ever known. The war, too, was coming to an end, and people were beginning to think about what the future might hold. When a depression or a war ends, it often marks important shifts in politics. Soldiers come home, workers return to their jobs, and beleaguered citizens increasingly come together to demand *never again!*

This was the context in which two important books appeared. Both were powerful and articulate, and written by thinkers of staggering intellect. Yet they contained opposing visions of what the world should look like.

Karl Polanyi's *The Great Transformation* argued that markets must always be regulated and embedded in social life, or they would come to destroy it. He called for an end to free markets and for the construction of democratic socialism.

Friedrich Hayek's book, on the other hand, argued for what we now call neoliberalism. Free markets, he wrote, were essential for individual liberty. He advocated a minimal state on the grounds that a large, activist state—at worst a socialist state—would inevitably send the country down a fearsome road to slavery. He titled his book *The Road to Serfdom.*

At the time, Hayek's vision was met with near total silence. The Great Depression had vindicated the ideas of left-wing thinkers like Polanyi and John Maynard Keynes, who insisted that unregulated markets led to disaster. The free markets of the 1920s, these thinkers noted, had led to the greatest inequality ever seen. On top of which, free markets had proven to be terribly unstable, leading to recession after recession, some minor, some devastating.

For many people, the Great Depression was the ultimate proof of the absurdity of free markets. Twelve million Americans, a quarter of the entire labour force, were left jobless. They desperately wanted to work, but were forced to starve right beside empty yet fully functioning factories. These factories were empty not because there was a shortage of workers or of potential consumers. There was an abundance of both. They were empty because businesses couldn't make a profit.

Eight thousand Americans committed suicide in the first year of the Depression alone.[1] In the richest country in the world, people were reduced to living in shantytowns. These encampments were called Hoovervilles after President Herbert Hoover, who, out of respect for free markets refused to intervene to stop the Depression. One report from Chicago in 1932 describes men, women, and children foraging through garbage dumps with sticks or their bare hands, seeking bits of food and vegetables.[2]

As if this wasn't bad enough, the European experience had clearly shown how small a step it was from economic instability to political instability. Across Europe, and particularly in Germany, economic depression had all too quickly given rise to xenophobia, racism, and the Nazis. Hayek's words, preaching a return to a golden age of capitalism like the 1920s, could not have been further from the political mood of the time.

The world thus turned away from Hayek and free market capitalism. Following the Depression the United States elected Franklin Delano Roosevelt, who ushered in a New Deal to expand public works and reduce unemployment. After the war the United Kingdom elected the socialist Labour Party, which likewise promised increased regulation of the market, greater equality, and public services for all. Governments across the West said never again to depression. Never again would any citizen be allowed to starve; never again would the elderly die alone in their houses for want of medical care.

On the foundations of disgust at war and abhorrence at depression, the Western countries transformed themselves into welfare states. For the first time in history, a number of societies dedicated themselves to the proposition that there is a certain level below which no citizen would be allowed to fall. They guaranteed

- basic security, such as public health care, a welfare safety net, and pensions
- basic opportunities, such as public education
- basic rights, such as the right to unionize at work and collectively bargain for better wages and conditions

The United States lagged behind Canada and Western Europe in these initiatives, especially in its failure to implement public health care and to distribute services equally among the white and African-American population. But in the ups and downs of human history, the creation of the welfare state marks a peak of social achievement.

It's important to remember that these humane changes were only possible as part of a larger reorganization of the economy. In place of relatively free markets, the state took on a significant role in economic management—regulating markets, redistributing wealth, and ensuring full employment.

The 1940s to the 1970s are usually understood as a period of class compromise. Workers agreed to temper their demands for radical or revolutionary change. (This was a period in which the Soviet Union was at its height of prestige, having played a major role in defeating Adolf Hitler. Socialist parties were winning elections across the world.) In exchange employers agreed to allow incremental but continual improvements. They would allow wages to rise steadily, permit unions to form, and agree to pay higher taxes.

It would be the role of the state to oversee this compromise. The state kept the economy functioning near full capacity so that there was full employment, meaning that nearly everyone who wanted a job could get one. It redistributed wealth, mainly through progressive taxation, requiring the rich to pay a higher percentage of tax than the poor. And it used the increased tax revenues to pay for universal public services.

The results of this period—which the French call *Les Trentes Glorieuses* and others call Keynesianism—were staggering. These were the most economically successful years that capitalism, in its roughly two-hundred-year history, has ever known. Despite dire predictions from the right, the high taxes and government intervention did not lead to economic catastrophe. In fact, productivity rose faster than before or since.

Between 1950 and 1973, Western Europe's gross domestic product (GDP) grew an average of 3.9 percent per year, meaning that income was doubling every eighteen years. Full employment was reached, with unemployment staying at very low levels (often below 2 percent). Inequality dropped significantly as prosperity was shared more generally. For instance, in the United States before the Depression, the top 10 percent of the population controlled 45 percent of the nation's income. This figure fell to 35 percent, where it was stable until the end of the 1970s. Average wages

Keynesianism

The economic theory called Keynesianism is named after John Maynard Keynes, a British economist. This theory defined the social democratic class compromise of the 1940s to the 1970s.

The state, according to Keynes, must take an active role in managing national economies. In particular, it must manage the total amount of demand in the economy in order to keep employment high and inflation low.

The core idea is that in downturns the government must stimulate demand (by increasing spending or cutting interest rates) in order to get the economy out of recession. And when the economy is running too hot, and inflation is rising, the state must act to reduce demand (by cutting spending or raising interest rates).

increased dramatically, at the same time as the number of working hours dropped. Last but not least, opportunity massively expanded with the numbers of young Americans (aged 18–24) going to university jumping from 10 percent in 1945 to 40 percent by 1980.[3]

The Class Compromise

Capitalism, which in the 1930s and 1940s was widely thought to be on its deathbed, had been saved. Yet in one of history's great ironies, it was saved not by the die-hard capitalists, but rather by the progressives and socialist reformers.

Thus my parents' generation, the baby boomers who grew up in the West in the 1960s, inherited a world where, at least among the relatively privileged white majority, there was no real fear of unemployment. No one doubted that if they wanted a job they could get one. And everyone expected to end up richer than their parents.

Security, prosperity, and opportunity had become tangible prospects for large swaths of the population. What is more, the material freedom that came from secure employment and a social safety net laid the foundation for an expanding sense of cultural freedom. With less fear for their own futures, young people became more confident in their ability to think for themselves.

Women began to question their subordinate gender role. Black and white students became increasingly vocal in their opposition to racism and segregation. Students started questioning their parents' values (their Protestantism, their patriarchy, their respect for authority) as old-fashioned and square. They gave up doo-wop for rock and roll, the glass of whisky for the joint and the tab of LSD.

The cultural changes of the 1960s were dramatic. Young people said no to racial segregation, yes to women's liberation, no to the American invasion of Vietnam. The culmination of the student movement led to an inspiring vision of a radically different kind of society, a genuinely democratic society that they called a "participatory democracy." This vision was captured by the Port Huron Statement in the United States, where the demand for participatory democracy first hit the mainstream. The vision of a new and radical democracy was echoed by students across the West. In France, students organized a massive strike and occupation of their universities in the summer of 1968, almost bringing down the government. The 1960s thus marked an ideological upheaval and a cultural flourishing that would have been impossible without the material security of the underlying class compromise.

Yet all this time there remained a core of right-wing ideologues, including Hayek and Milton Friedman. These true believers in free markets continued trying to convince anyone who would listen that regulated markets and heavy state intervention would sooner or later lead to slavery, or at least to inefficiency and poverty.

While he was still in the political shadows, Hayek had set up the Mont Pelerin Society in 1947, an enormously influential group whose members would include Friedman and Ludwig von Mises. Over the years the society became an important network for right-wing intellectuals and a driving force behind the creation of conservative think tanks. For example, in 1973 the Heritage Foundation was set up by former Mont Pelerin president Edwin Feulner. Heritage would profoundly influence U.S. president Ronald Reagan's policies in the 1980s, and is still one of the most influential think tanks in the United States. Another influential Mont Pelerin member was Antony Fisher, who started 150 right-wing think tanks worldwide, including probably the most influential one in the United Kingdom, the Institute of Economic Affairs.

But for the moment, these intellectual currents remained swirling around in the background. And then in the 1970s, two crucial changes occurred.

First the class compromise that had held the system together slowly began to unravel. As unions had become stronger, workers began more and more to question their bosses' power. They demanded better regulations (such as maternity leave and health and safety protocols), longer paid vacations, and, perhaps most frightening to business owners, more involvement in decision-making. In an era of low unemployment, the usual disciplining

Liberals, Neoliberals, and Conservatives

Classical liberals—like John Locke, Adam Smith, and Jeremy Bentham—believe in free markets and minimal states. In our day, these beliefs are espoused by people like Friedrich Hayek and Milton Friedman, which is why they are called "neoliberals." Sometimes they are also called "conservatives," but this is less accurate. Although they are conservative economically, they are not necessarily conservative socially. Neoliberals often support gay marriage, abortion, immigration, and so on. The term "conservative" is best reserved for people, like the religious right wing, who are keen on "conserving" traditional values and religious norms. Conservatives usually support neoliberal economics, but neoliberals do not necessarily support conservative social values.

mechanism—the threat of firing—lost much of its potency since there were always other jobs to be found. Slowly, bit by bit, owners found it harder to get maximal effort out of their workers for minimal pay. Profits started to get squeezed. By 1975 the profit rate in the United States was only 60 percent of the 1968 level, the lowest it had been in forty years.[4]

This was a turning point. Business owners had never been particularly enamoured with the compromise to begin with. Many believed it gave workers too much say over a business they saw as rightly "theirs." They had been willing to put up with it so long as profits remained high, but as soon as profits fell, their rationale for sticking with the compromise evaporated. Employers started pushing back. They pushed back over wages and against unions, and they pushed back ideologically. More money started finding its way to right-wing think tanks and lobbyists. The right became more vocal with its calls to roll back the unions and get the state "off our backs" (by which they meant less regulation over businesses and less taxation).

The second big change in the 1970s was that the general economic situation took a turn for the worse. War in the Middle East sent the price of oil skyrocketing. Since oil is such an important commodity, the general price level of everything—inflation—started to rise, too. At the same time, unemployment rose. This combination of rising inflation together with rising unemployment was called "stagflation."

Stagflation, measured by the aptly named "misery index," was doubly hard on people. At the same time as many lost their jobs, the money that they did have no longer went as far. Stagflation shook the confidence of the population and provided a crucial ideological opening.

At this time most economists and influential policy makers were Keynesians. They believed that, for the sake of efficiency as well as for justice, markets couldn't be left to themselves but needed to be regulated by the state.

One of the core assumptions of Keynesianism is that inflation and unemployment generally move in opposite directions. Inflation rises when unemployment is very low. When everyone has a job, it's easier for workers to bargain for higher wages. This in turn leads to higher prices. Likewise you can usually lower inflation by increasing unemployment. (When more people are out of work, they will accept lower wages, so prices will fall). So inflation and unemployment tend to move in opposite ways. But all of a sudden, stagflation meant that both inflation *and* unemployment were rising. A basic prediction of the left seemed wrong, or at least in need of a different explanation.

Many people became convinced that there was a large hole in economic understanding. This is when Milton Friedman, who had been quietly working in the economics department at the University of Chicago, suddenly stepped out of the shadows. He claimed that he could fill the hole by providing an explanation of stagflation.

Friedman argued that the Keynesians were wrong: there was no tradeoff between inflation and unemployment. The crucial thing was to keep inflation low because it always had the potential of spiralling out of control. There is a technical name for this—the non-accelerating inflation rate of unemployment, or NAIRU—but the upshot was quite simple. The government, he claimed, simply cannot effectively reduce unemployment at all. If it tries it will only produce higher and higher levels of inflation. His conclusion was that the state should back off, focus narrowly on keeping inflation low, and otherwise just let the market work by itself.

Such an anti-government message—especially one that came wrapped in scientific-sounding authority with formulas and graphs—was music to the ears of business. Friedman became immensely famous, and his ideas swept through university departments, think tanks, and non-governmental organizations (NGOs). By the mid-1980s, economic departments in universities across Canada, the United States, and the United Kingdom were dominated by neoliberals. The Heritage Foundation was a household name. And powerful NGOs such as the International Monetary Fund (IMF) and the World Bank were led by neoliberals.

In retrospect, most Keynesians today think their model is still basically right. The 2008 economic crisis has vindicated the Keynesian belief about the need to regulate markets. More specifically, unemployment and inflation have generally continued to move in opposite directions. Rare exceptions like that of the 1970s, which Friedman seized upon, are likely caused by unusual events. In this case, war in Israel and oil embargoes in the Middle East caused a surge in oil prices, leading to high inflation even with the high unemployment.

The Turn of the Tide

So two factors caused the political tide to turn at the end of the 1970s. On the one hand, there was falling profits and increasing business dislike of the class compromise. On the other there was stagflation and an intellectual turn away from Keynesianism.

In 1979 Margaret Thatcher, who liked to cite Hayek's *Road to Serfdom*, was elected prime minister in the United Kingdom. She immediately went to war with the unions, ultimately defeating the U.K. miners' strike.

In the United States, Ronald Reagan was elected president in 1981. Throughout his two terms he cut taxes on the richest from 70 percent to 28 percent, the largest tax cut in history.[5] In the 2000s, George W. Bush continued to cut taxes, mainly for the wealthy. To see the magnitude of the Bush tax cuts, imagine the U.S. government suddenly making this announcement. "Over the next decade we will send a cheque of $500,000 to each of the richest individuals in society, that is, to members of the top 0.1 percent (who already earn an average of $3 million per year)." You might think that this would be seen as totally outrageous. Yet it actually happened. Such are the results of the Bush tax cuts initiated in 2001, which mainly benefited the top 1 percent and particularly the top 0.1 percent.[6]

Reagan also tackled high inflation with policies that purposefully created massive unemployment. While inflation hurts everyone, it is usually disliked most by bankers and people with large savings. To see why, put yourself in the shoes of a banker whose job is to lend money. You lend $10,000 to Ms. Smith. Today that money can buy, say, one car. At the end of the year, Ms. Smith pays back the $10,000 (plus an interest payment). However, if there has been substantial inflation, that $10,000 is now worth less (because the same car now costs, say, $11,000). So in terms of what you as a banker can actually buy, inflation has made you poorer.

Inflation eats up the real worth of money, which is nice for borrowers but terrible for lenders. For regular people, inflation is a nuisance. But at moderate levels it's not nearly as dangerous as unemployment. (It's not a huge deal if prices go up as long as wages are going up as well). In general, low unemployment is the priority for regular working people, whereas low inflation is the priority for financial elites.

Reagan was concerned only about inflation. In order to reduce inflation his government raised the interest rate to a devastating 20 percent in 1981. This high interest rate made it impossible for many businesses to afford the loans they needed to keep their firms going. Many were forced to close down or lay off tens of thousands of workers. Unemployment did slow inflation because unemployed workers preferred to take reduced wages over no wages. But it did so at a terrible cost. Joblessness skyrocketed and the union movement in the United States was decimated, falling from a high of 34 percent of the labour force in 1954 to only 18 percent by 1985.[7]

In fact, participation in unions declined significantly in every part of the world except southern Africa. By 1997 the membership level in British unions was the lowest it had been in sixty years. This general decline is so significant to the way our societies function

that British economist Henry Phelps Brown rightly called it the "counter revolution of our time."[8]

In addition, Thatcher and Reagan began attacking the welfare system. Poor people were no longer sympathized with as our neighbours who had fallen on hard times, but vilified as "welfare queens" and "parasites." Public services were gutted in some places and fully privatized in others. And so with the end of full employment, the decline of unions, and the undermining of the welfare system, labour's strength was broken and the class compromise destroyed.

Nothing illustrates the end of the Keynesian class compromise better than the two astounding images in Figures 1.1 and 1.2. Figure 1.1, Percent Growth in Productivity and Hourly Compensation in the U.S., compares worker productivity, or output, with average hourly wages. During the class compromise period wages rose in step with productivity. Increased productivity, in other words, was translated into shared prosperity for all. In the 1970s, where the two lines diverge, the compromise was broken. Productivity continued to increase but its fruits were no longer shared.

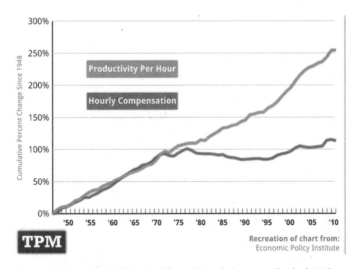

Figure 1.1 Percent Growth in Productivity and Hourly Compensation in the U.S.

Source: Brian Beutler, (2012). 40 Years of Workers Left Behind (CHART). Retrieved September 11, 2015, from http://talkingpointsmemo.com/dc/40-years-of-workers-left-behind-chart

The wages of average workers stagnated as the newly created wealth accrued entirely to the top. Over the last several decades the income of regular people has completely stagnated. In 1973 the average worker earned (adjusting for inflation) $22.41 per hour; by 2014 average pay was actually lower at $20.67 per hour.[9]

Figure 1.2, Income Inequality in the United States, illustrates this change in inequality. The late 1920s were the classic age of free markets and robber barons. Very high levels of income inequality were reached in the United States in the lead-up to the Great Depression. A massive reduction in inequality follows, during the Keynesian era. With the rise of neoliberalism in the 1970s, inequality begins to skyrockets once again. It returns in recent years to levels not seen since the late 1920s, with the top 10 percent receiving close to 50 percent of the nation's income.

Figure 1.2 Income Inequality in the United States, 1910–2010

Source: Thomas Piketty, *Capital in the Twenty-First Century*, trans. A. Goldhammer (Cambridge: Belknap, 2014), http://piketty.pse.ens.fr/en/capital21c2.

In both cases the explosive change that takes place in the 1970s is impossible to miss. Neoliberalism has arrived.

THE THREE PILLARS OF TINA

Throughout the 1980s neoliberalism continued to grow in strength. Thatcher and Reagan were re-elected, as was Canada's Progressive Conservative prime minister, Brian Mulroney. And then in 1989, much to everyone's amazement, the Berlin Wall fell, followed two years later by the total disintegration of the Soviet Union.

Since communism represented for many people the antithesis of free market capitalism, its fall made neoliberalism seemed invincible. The famous political scientist Francis Fukuyama summed up the neoliberal sentiment by declaring triumphantly that "history is over." To be fair, he did not believe that nothing would ever change. But what exactly did he mean? What precisely do neoliberals mean when they say *there is no alternative*?

Neoliberals like Friedman, Thatcher, Fukuyama, and others tend to sum up TINA in three main claims. TINA is like a giant dome supported by three pillars.

- Capitalism (by which they mean free markets with minimal state interferences) works well. It creates growth, prosperity, and freedom.
- The main historical alternative to capitalism—Soviet-style state communism—was a disaster. It was an authoritarian nightmare and incredibly inefficient, exemplified by the gulags on one side and the food queues on the other.
- The only other alternative—social democracy—is a failure, too. A heavy welfare state makes society rigid, leading to less freedom, less prosperity, and more entitlement seekers.

These have undeniably been influential ideas. Indeed, to a large degree they form the common sense of our time. This book is devoted to challenging these three claims. We will see that these pillars are not nearly as stable as they seem. The dome built on top of them—the whole edifice of TINA—is as fragile as a house of cards.

THE MEGAPHONE OF MYTHOLOGY

Over the last thirty or forty years TINA has become the dominant ideology of much of the world. Spreading from their birthplace in the University of Chicago, Wall Street, and the city of London, neoliberal ideas enveloped the world.

They transformed Russia through free market "shock therapy," transforming state ownership into free markets. This caused GDP to fall by 54 percent and the number of people living in poverty to skyrocket from 2 percent to 23 percent.[10]

In Latin America, the neoliberal focus on privatization, free trade, and reducing government intervention replaced state-led development models. This led in the 1980s to the "lost decade" of zero growth and enormous inequality, now the highest in the world.

In Africa, the story was a tragic one. After successfully overthrowing colonial governments in the 1950s and 1960s, many African nations were taken over by tyrants or military leaders who proceeded to borrow huge amounts of money from the West. This money was supposed to help develop their countries, but often ended up in the leaders' personal bank accounts, massively enriching themselves and their families. In the 1980s many of these countries found themselves in massive, unsustainable debt to Western banks. They found themselves with no choice but to beg the rich world for help. The World Bank, which provides loans to developing countries, would only help countries pay off their debts if they agreed to follow the neoliberal policies—called Structural Adjustment Programs—dictated by the International Monetary Fund.

These policies included privatizing water, lowering taxes on corporations and the rich, and reducing government spending on health care and food subsidies. And they caused the introduction of a new term—"IMF riot," a phenomenon that inevitably followed from the imposition of neoliberal policies. Between 1984 and 1990 the developing countries under Structural Adjustment Programs transferred $178 billion to Western commercial banks. So enormous was the capital sucked out of the Global South into the Global North that Morris Miller, former World Bank director, admitted, "Not since the conquistadors plundered Latin America has the world experienced such a flow in the direction we see today."[11]

One reason that neoliberal ideas were able to spread so far and so fast is that they were based on the idea that there is no viable alternative. TINA, in many ways, forms the backbone of neoliberalism. Today, if you ask a person on the street their thoughts about the future of capitalism, they will probably repeat some mantra about TINA.

How did it spread so far? How did it manage to become the common sense of millions of people? The answer is that ideas don't exist in a vacuum. Some ideas catch on because they're undeniably true. Some catch on because they resonate with the spirit of the times. And some ideas, because they align with powerful interests who promote them. The ideas of TINA have spread so far not because they are accurate; they have not become influential on the basis of their merits. But what the advocates of TINA lack in accuracy, they make up for in terms of power. TINA resonates with the interests of powerful, wealthy people in society, who use their power to amplify the idea far and wide. Wealth and power are the megaphones of the mythology of TINA.

How does this work? The most obvious way is through money. Money can buy many things in capitalist society, not least, the power to influence others. In Canada, for instance, the vast majority of media—the newspapers, TV shows, and radio programs—are privately owned and controlled by a small number of wealthy people. Six companies own about 90 percent of print, TV, satellite, and radio media.[12]

This is not to say that media owners are involved in any kind of conspiracy or secret plot. They don't meet in smoky rooms to maliciously slip quotes from Milton Friedman into the next day's editorial. They don't have to. The mechanisms at work are much simpler than that. Media owners naturally hire editors who are sympathetic to their views of the world.

For example, one family, the Asper family, until recently owned 89 percent of Canwest Global Communications. This media empire controlled a third of all Canadian newspaper circulation, including 11 large dailies and 120 local papers. In 2001 Canwest required every paper to print editorials written by the head office, which, due to Asper's personal politics, were pro-business, pro-free trade, and pro-Israel.[13]

Moreover, newspapers and online news sites are businesses whose main customers are other businesses looking to advertise. Online news sites make very little money selling news to individual readers; they make the bulk of their money on ads. Businesses placing ads are likely to share pro-business ideas of TINA too. So if media owners are going to have successful businesses, clearly they can't offend their advertising customers. Their businesses will do better if they reflect the world in a way that aligns with the values of their advertisers.

This is not conspiracy, it's just good business sense. It simply reflects the fact that owners of businesses have similar interests. They are all going to make more money if there is less tax, fewer regulations, and less union interference. This is no more mysterious than Manchester United players' common interest in winning soccer games. In similar social positions, it's normal for people to have similar perspectives.

An additional way that money can help to amplify ideas like TINA is through lobbying. In Canada, lobbying of politicians is somewhat restricted by the Election Expenses Act, which limits campaign contributions by citizens to $1,525, and bans unions and corporations from making any contributions.[14] In the United States, however, campaign contributions are basically a free-for-all. There are some limits to what can be given directly to individual politicians, but there are no limits on what can be given to shady "independent" organizations that indirectly support the politician. This means that corporations and rich individuals are allowed to give as much money as they like to promote politicians who are willing to stand up and extol neoliberal values.

The statistics are mind-blowing. In 2010, the average winning U.S. senator spent $9.8 million on their campaign. Indeed, of the sitting 435 House representatives, it is no accident that 402 outspent their opponent. The ramifications for democracy are clear, and depressing. These statistics mean that you cannot get elected on the basis of ideas and policies alone. The only way to get elected

The Tea Party: An Astroturf Movement

The U.S. Tea Party movement is a good example of the influence that money can have. Tea Party ideology is a mixed bag—conservative on social issues (anti-abortion, anti–gay marriage, anti-immigration) and neoliberal on economic values (free markets with minimal state interference and an extreme anti-tax position). In the 2010 midterm elections, the Tea Party stormed American politics, winning forty seats in the House of Representatives, many of which of which had been held by incumbents for years.*

How the Tea Party became so influential is a deeply instructive and scary story. From the beginning, the bulk of Tea Party events were sponsored by innocuous-sounding organizations, mainly FreedomWorks and Americans for Prosperity—both of which are funded by the billionaire Koch brothers. You can take practically any Tea Party event, any speech, any door-knocker, any paid activist, and if you follow their pay stubs, following the money back to the source, you will likely end up at the door of these two billionaire brothers in New York. (Koch Industries is the second-largest private corporation in the United States, involved in oil and chemical production, among other things). Ironically, this mostly working-class movement passionately demands lower taxes for the rich, against their own economic interests.

The Tea Party movement is really an "Astroturf" movement. It claims to be grassroots, but if you look closely enough you see that the grass is fake. It is bought, installed, and maintained by elites.

* Alexandra Moe, "Just 32% of Tea Party Candidates Win," NBC News, http://nbcnews.com, Nov. 3, 2010.

in the United States is to have bucketloads of money. And for most people, this means fundraising from corporations and wealthy individuals, who are going to be far more sympathetic to people promoting TINA than opposing it.

It's pretty rare for radical or socialist politicians to be invited to fundraising parties at the homes of millionaires. Raising inheritance taxes and democratizing businesses don't get discussed over champagne and the year's finest caviar. Of course, money can influence politicians from the both the left and the right. But it's a mistake to think that the influence is equally weighted. One of the sides has enormously more resources than the other. In fact, 70 percent of the donations that U.S. senators receive come from business, and only 6 percent from unions or labour representatives.[15]

There's another, deeper way that the mythology of TINA is spread. In 1982, Charles Lindblom at Yale, one of most respected political economists of the last fifty years, wrote an article describing the structure of the economy. The market system is a prison, he wrote, in the sense that it's very hard to escape from or change. Why? Because any attempt to introduce reforms that threaten profit levels tends to reduce private investment.

This is a problem because investment is the engine of the economic system. If businesses don't invest, the population won't have jobs. But businesses will only invest if they are confident that they will make a profit. Profits today are investments tomorrow, which are jobs the day after. Reforms that threaten profits tend to trigger collective punishments in the form of reduced investment—and therefore reduced jobs and a sluggish economy. Lindblom explained it this way:

> Do we want businesses to carry a larger share of the nation's tax burden? We must fear that such a reform will discourage business investment and curtail employment. Do we want business enterprises to reduce industrial pollution of

air and water? Again we must bear the consequences of the costs to them of their doing so and the resultant declines in investment and employment. Would we like to consider even more fundamental changes in business and market— worker participation in management, for example, or public scrutiny of corporate decisions? We can hardly imagine putting such proposals as those on the legislative agenda so disturbing would they be to business morale and incentive.[16]

In other words capitalism has a built-in defence mechanism. Attempts to reform it tend to hurt us all. This makes it very difficult to reform. It is an important reason why so many people are persuaded by TINA. Everywhere you look you see that attempts to implement change have the potential to backfire and hurt us all. This is the grain of truth within the husk of lies.

But we should not take it to mean that there are no alternatives. Lindblom himself is a democratic socialist who insists that quite radical changes are possible. To give just one example, it is often said that there is no alternative to current environmental policy—if you tax polluting businesses, jobs will be lost, and therefore TINA. Yet there are many possible responses. We could simply respond: *Okay, this is a worthwhile tradeoff. We will protect the environment and use state funding to retrain people in new, greener jobs.* Or we could implement subsidies to green businesses so that they can grow and create new jobs by outperforming the dirty firms. There is no shortage of good ideas about how to make reforms work. What we lack far more than good ideas is the conviction that real change is possible.

But even more fundamentally, the fact that the market does indeed resemble a prison in certain ways should not lead us to conclude that *there is no alternative.* Birmingham Jail in Alabama was a prison, but it couldn't contain Martin Luther King's dream of racial equality. Robben Island in South Africa was a prison, but after twenty-seven years the gates were opened, Nelson Mandela walked out, and apartheid fell. If the market is a prison, the appropriate response is not to say, *Oh well, it can't be changed.* A better response is: *We refuse to be prisoners of our economic system.*

An economic system that makes it harder to make things better is not a system that deserves to exist. The time has come to open the gates.

2

REALITIES OF
CAPITALISM I

INEQUALITY AND
WORKPLACE HIERARCHY

OUR CONTEMPORARY SOCIETIES are astronomically unequal. The 2011 Occupy Wall Street protests against economic injustice worked tirelessly to get this basic message out. The top 1 percent of the U.S. population controls 36.7 percent of all the wealth, whereas the bottom 40 percent own -0.9 percent (in other words, they don't own any wealth whatsoever, they're actually in debt).[1]

These statistics by themselves should be enough to make you feel a bit sick to the stomach. Let's imagine that every person in society is on a gigantic parade walking down the street, and each person's height represents their household income.[2] The average American has a family income of $68,000, so let's picture this person at the average height (and for simplicity, let's round it to 6 feet). Now imagine you're standing at the side of the road watching the whole society walk by in one hour. What will you see?

For the first 5 minutes everyone is less than 12 inches tall! At this stage the parade changes very slowly, with wave after wave of short people passing by. After 20 minutes a third of the parade is over, but you're still looking way down, as the marchers are only 3 feet tall. By about 40 minutes you're finally seeing people of average height. At 50 minutes people are about 9 feet tall. With only 10 minutes left of the parade things start changing very fast. At 54 minutes the people are 12 feet tall (twice the average income). At 57 minutes they are 16 feet tall. In the final 36 seconds the top 1 percent—the giants—start to pass by at a massive 35 feet tall ($400,000 income). In the last few seconds the top 0.1 percent appear at 140 feet tall, the height of a 14-storey building. In the last third of a second the super-rich—the top 0.01 percent, the CEOs and movie stars—pass by. They are 1,300 feet tall, as high as the tallest buildings on the planet (making $15 million). In the final micro-seconds the wealthiest pass by, earning around a billion dollars a year. They are a gargantuan 16 miles high—three times taller than Mount Everest!

As if it wasn't amazing enough, this parade actually understates the true inequality in U.S. society. It measures only annual income, not total accumulated wealth, which is significantly more unequal.

Worldwide, things are even worse: thirty thousand children die daily from poverty-related hunger and curable disease. That's ten times the number of people who died in the 9/11 terror attacks, every day. And yet there's no "war against poverty." Seven hundred million people live in extreme poverty—on less than $1.90 a day. Indeed, the world's sixty-two wealthiest people have the same amount of wealth as half of the entire world (3.6 billion people).[3]

WHAT'S WRONG WITH INEQUALITY?

This inequality is a terrible thing. It means that different individuals will have massively different opportunities and freedoms in their lives. This is why inequality is so unfair and so unjust. People in the same society, neighbours in the same city, people who are born and live and die in the same place have drastically different opportunities to live a good life.

Some have the means and resources to go to the schools they want, to get the jobs they desire, to achieve the goals they aspire to. Others—most—are denied the same opportunities. Their hopes are dashed and their dreams deferred. They are forced to live in insecurity and unpredictability—living lives, in the words of Henry David Thoreau, of "quiet desperation."

Inequality is a deep problem at both ends of the spectrum. For the poor, the impact is obvious. It means the inability to meet basic needs like housing, healthy food, health care. It means a lack of opportunities to develop one's capabilities and to flourish as a human being.

Moreover, inequality at today's level means that the rich are so powerful and wield so much influence that they undermine the basic functioning of our democracy. Can anyone really believe that the heart of democracy—that every citizen has an equal right to a say in how society operates—actually works in a society of tiny masses and a few isolated giants taller than mountains?

The evidence is overwhelming that inequality is terrible for society as a whole. For example, across the world, developed countries with higher inequality also have higher levels of mental illness, teenage pregnancy, obesity, incarceration, and homicides. They have lower levels of life expectancy, social trust, children's educational performance, and social mobility (that is, the ability to move up the ladder).[4]

So inequality is not just a problem for the poor: it is a societal disaster. Beneath the statistics, inequality represents a slow and painful tearing of the social fabric. The more that people living side by side become unequal, the more they begin to inhabit different social groups and to live in different worlds. As this happens, it becomes harder and harder to experience a real sense of community and empathy, making society less cohesive, less solidaristic, and less stable.

One obvious example is the American prison system, where a huge number of poor and mainly racialized people end up. On any given day, about one-third of all African-American men in their twenties are behind bars, on probation, or on parole. As philosopher Brian Barry notes, this rate of incarceration for blacks is "higher than the total incarceration rate in the Soviet Union at the zenith of the gulag and in South Africa at the height of the anti-apartheid struggle."[5]

The more that different groups grow apart, the more likely it is that the rich will look down at the rest of us with contempt, and everyone else will look up at them with resentment. Distrust and hatred grow "like a fungus" in the social cleavages between the rich and poor.[6] This is not a recipe for a happy society.

Now, the standard capitalist myth is that inequality is not a problem because the system is fair. The usual defence of inequality, parroted every day by Fox News, *The Wall Street Journal,* and others, goes something like this. The market is a competition, like the 1,500-metre race. We all start our working lives from the same starting line, and the winner of the race gets lots of money. Some people train hard, run fast, and make millions. Others, who are unfit and lazy, run slowly and make nothing.

This message gets drilled into us every day. It's the essence of the American dream. Everyone has the same chance, and if you try hard you can be successful and become rich. In other words, you get what you deserve. That's why if anyone tries to take away your winnings, it would be unfair.

Translated into political language, the idea is that capitalism provides equal opportunity. The income you receive is fair, because it depends entirely on the effort you have made. Those who work harder rightly make more, while those who are poor have no one to blame but themselves. Moreover, taxation is theft. It involves the government taking what is rightfully *mine*.

This argument will likely sound familiar. But in fact it is wrong—utterly wrong. In reality the race is fixed. It is rigged in such a way that some people are propelled forward while others are held back. In a capitalist market, there is almost no connection between what people rightfully deserve and what they actually earn.

Although there are philosophical debates about it, for the sake of argument let's accept the basic moral principle that underlies the American dream: the amount of income that people deserve depends on the effort they put in. The reality is that what people actually get in capitalism has little to do with personal effort. It has almost everything to do with how lucky they are to be in a strong bargaining position in the market.

In real life people aren't running in a fair race, nor do they get to the finish line by relying purely on their own effort. Some are pushed forward and some are held back. The American dream is a lie because people have very unequal opportunities.

But don't take my word for it. Let's look at the evidence.

THE STARTING LINE

Even before birth, inequality affects opportunity. The mother's health affects the development of the fetus. So a mother who has inadequate nutrition, medical care, and social supports is less likely to give birth to a healthy baby. A family that is well off is likely to pass on health advantages from day one.

Next, richer families are better able to nurture and educate their young children. Indeed, sociologists have shown that a gap in education between richer and poorer children is visible as early as twenty-two months. One American study found that "the average (rounded) number of words children heard per hour was 2,150 from professional families, 1,250 in the working-class families and 620 in the welfare families."[7] This is mainly because wealthier families can afford to have stay-at-home parents providing lots of one-on-one time with the child or can afford to pay for good, attentive childcare. So already at this age, rich kids are starting to move further ahead.

The differences in opportunities grow starker as the years go by. Wealthier families may send their kids to private schools, where they are in smaller classes and receive more personal support. Poorer kids often go to school in rougher neighbourhoods, with bigger classes and more stressed out teachers. Some students may not be fed well enough to concentrate. The poorest public schools in the United States receive only $3,000 per student, whereas the wealthiest private schools in New York City can cost up to $40,000 per year.[8]

By the time students finish high school, the difference in abilities is massive. And it appears starkly along class and race lines. For example, in the United States in 1999, the average score in mathematics for a 17-year-old black kid was 283.3, almost exactly the same as the average score for a 13-year-old white kid (283.1). In the United Kingdom, a middle-class kid is a whopping fifteen times more likely to stay at that level than a working-class kid is to become middle-class.[9]

By our mid-teens, then, some of us already have much more opportunity than others. To return to the racing analogy, some runners are getting years of workouts, professional training, and dietary supplements long before the race to make money has even started. These advantages are totally undeserved. There is no real question of "effort" here.

School-age children can't really be blamed or praised as autonomous individuals for how well they do in school. That depends hugely on luck: how much social support they get from parents and teachers, how safe their neighbourhoods are, how much gang activity and violence they experience, and so on. Hard-working kids will do better than slackers. But the most hard-working kid in the world is unlikely to do as well academically in a rundown overpopulated school in the inner city than a slacker does in an elite prep school in the wealthy suburbs.

The gap in opportunity widens even further when these teens graduate and make a decision about getting a job or going to university. At the moment, some teenagers—but only a privileged few—get to go to elite universities. For example, the cost of doing an undergraduate degree at an Ivy League school in the United States is approximately $200,000 (tuition plus room and board for a four-year degree). Canadian schools are somewhat more accessible, but they can still be extremely expensive. A three-year law degree at the University of Toronto currently costs C$99,000.

Clearly only a fraction of the population can afford it. But if your parents are rich enough to send you to a prestigious university, your future is looking pretty good.

Someone might argue, if you sacrifice seven or eight years working hard at university to get a professional degree in law or medicine, don't you deserve to earn a lot of money? After all, you're doing a job that no one else could do.

This is a common perspective, but it doesn't really hold up. First of all, it's hard to say with a straight face that going to university is a sacrifice. The fifteen hours of class per week, the parties, the meeting of new people and discovery of new ideas—that's not exactly working in the mines. Anyone with a bit of humility knows that going to university is not a sacrifice but a privilege. Ask a grandparent who wasn't able to go. It's a bit of a joke for middle- and upper-class medical students to look down on working-class people and say, "Even though you had to leave school to get a job at seventeen, I'm making a sacrifice by going to medical school, where I get to learn amazing things and develop skills that everyone admires."

Second, the reason that doctors and lawyers get paid so much is not primarily because of their skill. Plumbers, electricians, bakers, nurses, and all kinds of people have particular skills, too. The difference is that there is no level playing field between these professions. The number of doctors and lawyers is strictly limited by the government. That's why so many well-trained immigrant doctors in North America are forced to drive cabs. Since the supply is kept so low, professionals can demand very high wages. If everyone with the requisite grades who wanted to could attend medical school, the number of doctors would explode and the wages would plummet.

It's not necessarily a bad policy to regulate the number of positions for these jobs; that's a separate question. But there is nothing "natural" or "deserving" about their high pay. It's an artificial result of structuring a particular labour market in a particular way.

By the time people leave university and are ready to start applying for jobs—by the time the "race" is about to start—the opportunities available to them are massively different. And those opportunities are made even more unequal by the fact that some people inherit huge amounts of money. Most of the richest people in society have not earned their money at all—they simply inherited it. For example, of the richest four hundred people on the *Forbes 400* list, 21 percent simply inherited all their wealth and fully 60 percent of the people on the list started life with about $1 million.[10] These people start the race at the finish line. Their success requires no effort or talent or risk-taking.

Even the most devout capitalist will find it hard to argue that millionaire babies deserve their wealth. Did they swim extra hard out of the birth canal? No. They were simply lucky to be born into a rich family.

Put all of this together—the health of the parents, the quality of the learning environment and the neighbourhood, the schools and universities, the unearned inheritances—and what you get is clear. Systemic advantage for some and systemic disadvantage for others. The overarching fact is that if you're born in Charlotte, North Carolina, in the bottom 20 percent of society, what are the chances that you'll ever reach the top 20 percent? Four percent.[11]

The vast majority of all of this is brute luck. The factors that play such a large role in determining your bargaining power as you enter the market to look for a job depend almost entirely on luck, not personal effort. And so, the income that is made from such a position can hardly be said to be morally deserved.

Consider this: a black man in the United States has a life expectancy of 71.8 years, 4.7 years less than the average for white men. Likewise, an indigenous male in Canada has a life expectancy of 64 years, which is 15 years less than the Canadian male average.[12] How can we explain these striking differences? There are only two ways to explain why black and indigenous people die so young: a racist explanation that places the blame on them for not trying hard enough, or an accurate explanation that recognizes the huge societal barriers and obstacles they face every step of the way.

If you're still not convinced, ask yourself this. What would you guess is the single most important factor in determining how much money you will make in your life? Is it effort, talent, the university you go to, the amount you inherit? In fact, the single most important factor, bar none, is the country you are born into. According to World Bank economist Branko Milanovic, place of birth explains more than 60 percent of the variability of people's incomes. For example, only 3 percent of Indians will end up richer than the poorest 1 percent of Americans. So even if an American spent their life in total indolence, developing no skills, exerting no effort, and making no contribution to the economy, they would still be richer than 97 percent of Indians. Milanovic's conclusion is that "most of one's lifetime income will be determined at birth."[13]

Here's another example. A bus driver in Sweden makes nearly fifty times more than one doing the exact same job in India. According to capitalist orthodoxy, this must be because the Swedish driver works fifty times harder. That is absurd. If anything it's likely that the Indian driver works harder; the evidence shows that people in poorer countries generally work longer hours and are more entrepreneurial than people in richer countries. They have to, in order to survive.[14] The reason that Swedish drivers make so much more has nothing to do with their effort. It has to do with their good luck in working in a rich country where they are able to profit from society's resources. Yet no one chooses where they are going to be born. So no one can say that they actually deserve the bulk of their income.

Let's take a step back to put this all in perspective. Capitalists try to sell us an image that life in the job market is like a running race around a track. But a much more accurate image is of a vehicle race. In reality, the market is like a race around a racetrack where everyone starts at the same line (there is no official discrimination on the basis of race or sex), yet some people race on rollerblades, some on skateboards, some on bikes, some on motorbikes, some in normal cars, and some in very expensive professional Grand Prix race cars. Every time you do a lap around the track you get paid depending on your position—the winners make the most, the losers the least.

The race isn't literally fixed. There's still room for chance and effort to play a role, and hard work can make a difference. But what will be the results? It seems pretty obvious. Those who were lucky enough to start the race in powerful vehicles will move further and further ahead as the race goes on. They will make more money with each lap, regardless of how desperately hard the skateboarders try. That is the reality of neoliberal capitalism. Whatever else may be said about it, it is hard to call it fair.

This is why the idea of the "self-made man," people who have pulled themselves up by their own bootstraps is, by and large, such nonsense. It's why the American dream, though a beautiful idea, is such a sham in practice. Indeed, this is part of the reason why the radical civil rights leader Malcolm X famously said, "I don't see any American dream; I see an American nightmare."[15] This is why it's so gross when rich people talk about "individual responsibility" while looking down their noses at others.

"I got where I am through hard work," they say. "If you're poor you must be lazy; you should smoke and drink less and work more…"

When they talk like this they are ignoring all the myriad advantages they have received, as well as the multiple disadvantages that others have suffered. They are lying about the amount of help they have received and blaming the victim for the help they didn't receive.

No one gets where they are purely by themselves. We are social creatures. We depend on others for nurturing, facilitating, teaching, mentoring, and aiding us every step of the way. Unfortunately, in our present society, some of us receive much more social support than others. Much of this support—particularly the caring and nurturing work, performed overwhelmingly by women—

The Richest Woman in the World

Gina Rinehart is the richest woman in the world. She is the owner of Hancock Prospecting, a mining company set up by her father on the basis of iron and coal deposits in western Australia that he claimed to discover. She has an estimated net personal wealth of $29.3 billion (it is said that she makes roughly $600 every second).* She is well known for telling others that they could be rich too if only they worked harder: "If you're jealous of those with more money, don't just sit there and complain; do something to make more money yourself—spend less time drinking, or smoking and socializing, and more time working."† She has been calling for a reduction in the minimum wage and recently told her fellow Australians that they should look to the "Africans . . . willing to work for less than $2 per day" as inspiration.‡

But even though Rinehart talks a lot about "hard work" and individual responsibility, the truth is that she inherited basically all of her wealth. (The day she became old enough to drive, her father bought her ten brand new cars to choose her favourite from).§ Since her father gave her the company, she has been receiving royalty cheques worth millions of dollars every year. Of course she never actually worked in a mine; she simply sits in her boardroom and receives the dividend payments. But at the same time she has no problem telling the miners doing the actual work that they should take a pay cut and work harder.

* "Australia's Gina Rinehart Is 'World's Richest Woman,'" BBC, www.bbc.com, May 24, 2012.

† Joshua Berlinger, "World's Richest Woman Tells Jealous People to Drink Less and Work More," *Business Insider*, www.businessinsider.com, Aug. 30, 2012.

‡ Duncan Kennedy, "Gina Rinehart Calls for Australian Wage Cut," BBC, www.bbc.com, Sept. 5, 2012.

§ William Finnegan, "The Miner's Daughter," *The New Yorker*, March 25, 2013.

exists in the background, in the shadows of the private family. That makes it is easy for certain individuals, especially powerful men, to ignore all the care they have received and claim they got where they are all by themselves.

DISTRIBUTING THE WEALTH

In our current economy, individual effort plays a much smaller role than the kind of opportunities you have—the "vehicle" you get to race in. A decent society, on the other hand, would create an economy where everyone had real equal opportunity.

Once we realize the brutal unfairness in our economy, we see that anger toward taxation is misplaced. Decent people should call for much higher levels of taxation. Of course, sometimes governments waste tax dollars, or spend them on things we need less of—like armies. But if that happens, it's the fault of unaccountable governments or bad priorities. It's not a problem with taxation itself.

High redistributive taxation will do two things. It will reduce the current unfairness of unequal opportunities. And it will pay for building up a society of genuinely equal opportunity so that poor kids get the same opportunities as rich kids. Taxes can fund free daycare, good parental leave, good public schools, free university, universal health care, and so on. In other words, we should start giving some of the winnings of the race car drivers to the people on skateboards, and start providing equal vehicles for everyone to race in. We need to create a society of genuine opportunity so that everyone can access the things they need to flourish as human beings.

That's why we should be on the streets demanding very high taxation. If we're serious about social justice, we should call for something like a 99 percent inheritance (and gift) tax, as well as a 90 percent income tax for people earning over, say, $10 million a year. These numbers sound much higher than we're used to hearing, but they aren't unreasonable. It's just that the neoliberal myth of TINA has convinced people that taxing the rich is wrong. So I want to point out why taxation is fully justified—indeed, desperately needed.

The first thing to appreciate is that taxation is not theft, it's rent. Taxation is the way that we pay society back for being allowed to use its resources. Let's compare a corn farmer in Canada to an imaginary farmer on a deserted island. How much income is each going to be able to generate? The farmer on the deserted island has nothing to use but their hands. They must pull up the weeds with their fingers and try to make a plough out of fallen branches. They have to rely on the rain to water the crops, and so on. So they'll maybe be able to grow a hundred ears of corn. The Canadian farmer, on the other hand, can go to a bank to get a loan. Then they can buy fertilizer and a powerful tractor with which they can plough large expanses of land, growing perhaps ten thousand ears of corn.

The crucial thing to realize is that the Canadian is ending up so much richer not because of personal effort—if anything they're working *less* hard—but because they can draw on the massive resources of their society. They are drawing on banks, technology, factories that produce tractors, and so on. If personal effort by itself can grow a hundred ears of corn, but the Canadian farmer ends up with ten thousand, then this means that the vast majority of their income (99 percent in this example) isn't due to effort. The real source of the vast majority of our income is the society in which we live.

So taxation is not theft. It's simply the rent we pay society back for the privilege of using its resources and the amazing technical and material wealth it has developed over the years. Only someone who has never used society's resources could justly complain that tax is theft. A person who has never used a road, drunk tap water, plugged in an appliance, been educated in a school or treated in a hospital, used bills or coins printed by the government, or benefited from generations of collective knowledge and technology. In other words, no one.

The father of the Microsoft billionaire Bill Gates put it this way: "Success is a product of having been born in this country, a place where education and research are subsidized, where there is an orderly market, where the private sector reaps enormous benefits from public investment. For someone to assert that he or she has grown wealthy in America without the benefit of substantial public investment is pure hubris."[16]

The second reason to support high taxation is justice. The political philosopher Thad Williamson points out that if the United States redistributed only 30 percent of the wealth of the top 1 percent (allowing them to retain most of their gigantic wealth), we could ensure that every household would have at least $100,000 in assets.[17] A good society would set its taxes high enough to reduce the unequal opportunities that currently exist, in order to provide real equal opportunities for everyone. No one really makes their money all by themselves. Our income comes from our society— it's a kind of social inheritance. That's why it's fair to have to pay a bunch of it back for the next generation.

Of course rich people will complain that taxation diminishes their freedom. But redistributive taxation doesn't reduce freedom, it just shifts freedoms around. While the rich will have fewer opportunities to sail their yachts or fly their personal airplanes, the poor will have more opportunities to get good health care, go to good schools and universities, and so on. That's not a reduction of freedom; it's an increase in the kind of freedoms that really matter.

Neoliberals also object to taxes on practical grounds of incentives. They argue that if taxes are high, people will lose their motivation to work hard, and this will mean that society as a whole will end up poorer. Now, it's true that taxes *might* cause incentive problems, but there is no guarantee that they would. First, higher taxes might just as well make people work harder (since longer hours are needed to make the income that one is aiming for). Second, there is no incentive problem for inheritance tax (since the person is dead). Third, if the majority of society believes the tax levels are just, then there will be no change in motivation. For example, during the Second World War, the United States had top income tax rates above 90 percent without any problems (since everyone agreed that the taxation was for an important collective cause).

Finally, even people like me who believe that equal opportunity is extremely important do not think that we need taxes to ensure total equality. It's easy to imagine a system where the largest allowable gap between highest and lowest pays is something like 3 to 1 or maybe even 10 to 1. That would be a tremendous amount of equality compared to today. Yet it would still provide significant motivation for those who feel that they'll only work hard if they can end up with more than their neighbours.

EXPLOITATION IN THE WORKPLACE

What about the workplace? Once you find yourself looking for a job, how fair an environment can you expect to find?

A year ago, my friend Saani moved to Toronto from Ghana to start a new life. A middle-class civil servant back home, he arrived in Canada bursting with talent, energy, and determination to succeed. Yet within a couple of months, his friends and family in Africa were growing increasingly perplexed. Why wasn't he sending back lots of money? Why wasn't he rich yet? After all, he had *made it*. He had successfully got to Canada without being thrown into jail by immigration authorities. He had entered the rich world, with the skyscrapers, mansions, and shopping malls, where the average person has more money than most Ghanaians could ever dream of. So what was the problem?

After visiting employment centre after employment centre, willing to take anything, the first job Saani was offered was in a tire factory. It was in the outskirts of the city, an hour's bus ride away. The company had only one job on offer: night shift from midnight to 8 a.m., standing on his feet on an assembly line. The job was a nightmare. He had to perform the same repetitive action again and again, all night long. The mind-numbing dullness was offset only by increasingly sharp pains shooting up his legs from standing still for so long. The supervisor walked around yelling abuse at the workers to work faster and not take such long bathroom breaks.

The job paid minimum wage—C$11 an hour. Saani told me that none of the workers could bear it for more than several months. He became increasingly depressed. This was a far cry from the capitalist paradise he had expected to find in Canada.

The capitalist myth is that work is a free and fair exchange of labour for money. That is how the typical job contract is understood by two of the most famous neoliberal economists in this area, Armen Alchian and Harold Demsetz. First, they insist that job contracts are free because they are voluntary. No one forces anyone to sign a contract. On the contrary, the worker and "the employer [are] continually . . . involved in renegotiation of contracts on terms that must be acceptable to both parties."

Second, Alchian and Demsetz insist that contracts are fair because they happen between equals, so there is no issue of power or hierarchy at work. The firm "has no power . . . , no authority, no disciplinary action any different in the slightest degree from ordinary market contracting between any two people." Indeed, "the employee 'orders' the owner . . . to pay him money in the same sense that the employer directs . . . [the employee] to perform certain tasks. The employee can terminate the contract as readily as can the employer."[18]

Let's examine the issue a bit more closely. First, is it right to say that the work contract is really free and voluntary? As we have seen, our society is one of extreme inequality. Some people have lots of money and own their own private businesses, while most don't. The only thing most people have to sell is their labour. That's what it means to be an ordinary working person. We can't simply live off our investments; we have to rent out our labour to make ends meet.

If we think about my friend Saani, it's true that he is legally free to quit whenever he wants. It's also true that he chose to sign a contract; no one put a gun to his head. But Alchian and Demsetz's claim that Saani is just as free to fire the boss as the boss is to fire him is pretty laughable. Saani needs the job. He has no alternatives. He has to find a job now in order to pay the rent next month. The boss, on the other hand, doesn't need him. The company has plenty of workers to choose from and plenty of money saved up. If a worker quits it might be a minor inconvenience, but it's not a big deal.

Of course, it's possible for Saani to refuse work and rely on welfare. But the current welfare rates in Toronto are an appalling C$657 per month, while the average one-room apartment costs C$1,123.[19] This is an incredibly unattractive option. So while no one held a gun to Saani's head to take this job, he was coerced by the system in general. He has to work or else he'd suffer serious deprivation.

This means that Alchian and Demsetz have mistaken the formal freedom to quit whenever one wants with the reality that for most people this is not an easy option. Most people are forced to work. They apply for jobs with few alternatives and from a position of much less bargaining power than their employers. They are largely compelled to take what's offered.

What is work like in our society? What is the essence of the workplace in capitalist society? Of course every workplace is different. Some bosses are jerks and some are genuinely nice people. But the crucial thing to realize about businesses in capitalist society is that they are places of antagonistic class interests. No matter how nice the boss is as an individual, in their role as a boss their interests are the exact opposite of their workers. This is one of the great tragedies of capitalism. It forces even kind and generous business owners to act in mean and exploitative ways. If a boss at one firm is more lenient than the next, their firm will make less money and eventually they'll be driven under by the competition.

Think about work in any kind of business—an office, a store, a factory. I like the example of a restaurant, since it was while washing dishes that I had my first realizations about capitalism. My basic epiphany is kind of obvious in retrospect, but it took me a while to work out. I had the exactly opposite interests as my boss.

If I worked extra hard scrubbing the dishes, at the end of the day it would be the boss, not me, making more money. The more effort I put in, the more that they got out. The boss wanted me to work harder and get paid less; I wanted to work less hard and get paid more. This is the fundamental antagonism, the unsolvable clash of interests, at the heart of every capitalist business.

This antagonism ripples throughout society. The core of the antagonism is the opposing interests regarding wages and effort. But you also see it in terms of benefits, vacation time, and sick pay. Workers want more, employers want less. Likewise in rules and regulations about safety, hazards, overtime, and so on. Workers want more regulations to protect themselves, employers want less to make more money. Workers want more parental leave, employers want less. Workers want steady yet flexible hours, while bosses want to be able to call a worker in or send them home at any moment.

This antagonism explains why management so often hates unions. It explains why Walmart will go so far as to fire any worker even breathing the words "collective bargaining."[20] It explains why employers have pumped so much money over the years into publicity campaigns trying to discredit unions as corrupt and unnecessary. Employers don't necessarily act in exploitative ways because they're bad people. But the basic class conflict means that the more unions protect workers, the harder a time employers will have making a profit. A close friend of mine got fired recently for trying to unionize her workplace—at a social justice charity! Though clearly one that saw itself first and foremost as a business.

More broadly, the antagonism at the heart of all capitalist businesses requires employers to discipline their workers. Disciplined workers mean steady, predictable profits. The first source of discipline that employers look to is external. It comes from having a sizable chunk of the population unemployed. A reserve body of desperate, unemployed workers dramatically increases employers' bargaining power and ability to discipline their workers. In such an environment, they are able to demand more effort and lower wages. Any resistance can be met by simply firing the worker and hiring an unemployed person who is likely to be grateful for any job whatsoever.

In other words, the threat of unemployment is the basic disciplinary measure at the employer's disposal. This is why the president of General Electric recommended automatically firing 10 percent of the company's employees every year in order to keep the others in check.[21] It is also the reason we see so much resistance to welfare in our societies, particularly in the right-wing press. If financial assistance rates are high enough, they start to dull the threat of unemployment and undermine the bosses' power. Battles over the unemployment level and welfare rates are so contentious because they represent flip sides of the same coin—the relative power of workers versus bosses.

The second major source of discipline that employers use is internal—the hierarchical management. In Alchian and Demsetz's classical analysis, the purpose of a firm's management is to be able to constantly monitor each worker's effort, so as "to discipline and reduce shirking."[22] Or, more straightforwardly, to keep the workers in a state of fear. In addition, the carrot can be just as effective as the stick. This is why small promotions and occasional raises are so useful—they keep workers submissive and hard-working. But ultimately, the central purpose of management is to extract as much effort from as little wages as possible.

For 150 years socialists have had a word for this: exploitation. Indeed, the whole history of management techniques—whether it's brutal yelling and screaming, kind coaxing and calling the firm a "family," or supplying the workers with bottomless coffee—all aim at the same thing, maximizing profits. The evolution of management techniques is little more than the science of exploitation.

HIERARCHY IN THE WORKPLACE

Workplace management brings us to the second major claim of Alchian and Demsetz—that the workplace is really an egalitarian space, with no power and no authority. This argument clashes with common sense and everyday experience.

Think for a moment about what workplace hierarchy is like for the majority of the population. The most common jobs in capitalist societies today are retail and service jobs, for example in department stores.[23] Often in these jobs, workers find themselves ordered around by the manager, given menial, repetitive tasks day in, day out. They have little say in the running of the store, ability to influence its direction, or voice in its organization. They may be given small responsibilities, but essentially being a worker (as opposed to a manager) generally means being a decision-follower. It means that workers' own initiatives tend to be ignored or undermined, and their human talents and potential tend to be deprecated in favour of their machine-like abilities to follow orders.

Some firms, like Walmart, may be particularly harsh—forcing overtime and forbidding breaks.[24] But even companies that aren't so cold-hearted are structured as hierarchies. Almost everyone has experienced at some time or another the degradations of workplace hierarchy. Yelling bosses, managers who act like petty tyrants, supervisors who stonewall and stifle feedback, arbitrariness and inequality, favouritism and snobbery, privilege and superiority. Workplace hierarchy undermines the freedom of working people to be in control of their own lives.[25]

Capitalist workplaces are hierarchical not because the bosses and managers are necessarily mean people. Some are, some aren't. They are hierarchical because that's the basic structure of work in our societies.

When workers starts a new job they sign a contract. Since most workers come in with far less bargaining power than the employer, the typical contract (for low- and medium-skilled work) gives large discretionary power to the employer over the employee. It's impossible for a contract to spell out in detail every task that must be performed. So what such contracts really establish is the authority of bosses to govern their workers. Contracts give employers the power to tell workers to do this task in that way.

Hierarchy vs. Democracy

In a hierarchy, power and authority reside in a pyramidal structure or chain of command, unaccountable to those below. Distinct ranks of people acquire different material, moral, and/or cultural privileges. Examples include states (like apartheid South Africa, or contemporary Burma), traditional armies and militaries, *and conventional capitalist firms.*

Democracy, by contrast, is an organizational structure in which ultimate authority resides in the collective membership. Those at the highest level are elected by and fundamentally accountable to those below. Examples include democratic governments as well as co-operative firms. These structures often involve different amounts of authority at different levels, but all such authority is ultimately accountable to the members.

While some on the left have historically focused on exploitation at work, others have focused more on the domination that goes along with hierarchy—the relations of power and subservience that exist between workers and bosses. To make a broad generalization, the analysis of exploitation stems mainly from the Marxist tradition. Anarchists have tended to accept a lot of this analysis but usually want to expand the focus of oppression beyond exploitation to talk about domination. Domination can include class, but is a broader category including gender, race, sexuality, ability, immigration status, and so on. For an interesting discussion on the pros and cons of these approaches, see M. Bookchin, *Anarchism, Marxism, and the Future of the Left* (San Francisco: A.K. Press, 1999).

The contract establishes the worker as essentially a tool—a piece of clever machinery that will do what it is told. This is why workplace hierarchy can often feel so degrading.

Some workplaces may be outright oppressive and others have a friendlier atmosphere. But every capitalist workplace has a governance structure that institutionalizes inequality, giving those at the top unaccountable power over those at the bottom. For those of us on the left, workplace hierarchy is inherently objectionable. It strikes us as deeply and disturbingly undemocratic. The more you think about it, the more bizarre it seems that we let businesses be undemocratic.

Consider the following common situation: Joan decides that she wants to retire, and so she gives the company to her son, Mark. All of a sudden Mark is in charge. He may have never set foot in the business before and may know nothing about it. But he strolls in on Monday morning, twenty years younger than all the workers, with the power to hire and fire, to give raises and slash pensions. He orders the workers to change the business direction, scrapping a project that they have been working on for years to take up an entirely different one. Perhaps he insists on a more formal workplace than his mother did—requiring the workers to dress differently and refer to him as "sir."

We immediately feel the injustice of such a situation because we see that what is being inherited here is not simply wealth but power. Yet in a democratic society, power over other human beings should never be inherited. That's what it means to have evolved beyond the feudalism of the Middle Ages. As we now recognize, power over others is illegitimate and tyrannical unless it is accountable to the people affected by it.

Although our societies in the West take it for granted that workers don't elect their bosses, it's actually a very strange thing. We call ourselves democracies, yet most of us spend the bulk of our lives—forty hours a week for years and years—in undemocratic organizations. There is a massive gap between our democratic rhetoric and our democratic reality.

In the last couple of centuries, democracy has slowly gained a grip on people's hearts and minds. This spirit of equality was resisted by kings and aristocrats, priests and slave-owners. But slowly democratic rights spread, first to propertied men, then after the French Revolution, to all men. The suffragette movements of the early 1900s spread democratic rights to women, and finally in the 1950s and 1960s, African-Americans in the United States and indigenous people in Canada were included.

The spread of democracy has been one of the great successes of human emancipation. But in recent years, it has been firmly blocked by the closed gate of the factory. The tide of democracy rose steadily for two hundred years until it crashed into the rocks of economic power. Today we are left with the paradox of a democratic society in which one of the most important institutions of all—the workplace—remains staunchly undemocratic.

A striking illustration of this paradox is the example of Pullman, Illinois.[26] In the late 1800s, George Pullman was the owner of a very successful railroad carriage company. Then, as now, the mainstream opinion was that there was nothing wrong with him controlling the firm and directing the workers. But in 1880 Pullman built a town in Illinois to house his workers, and named it after himself. It had all the usual amenities—stores, churches, entertainment facilities, and so on—with the unusual feature that Pullman owned the town and everything in it. Workers had to live in his houses and abide by his rules. For example, Pullman unilaterally decided to ban alcohol from the town.

This struck many people as unacceptable, undemocratic, even tyrannical. But Pullman pointed out that it was unclear what people objected to. His authority over the workers at the workplace was justified by the free contracts the workers had signed, the use of his own money, the risks he has taken building up the business, his entrepreneurial zeal. And all of these factors were exactly the same in the case of the town.

Eventually the U.S. Supreme Court forced Pullman to cede the town to Chicago, declaring that ownership of a community was "incompatible with the theory and spirit of our institutions." In other words, the Supreme Court declared that it is undemocratic and unacceptable for an individual to control a political community. But they could not provide any real reason why. Why is unaccountable power permitted in a firm but not in a town? Why is it acceptable in an economic community but not a political one? Why do towns need to be democratic but workplaces do not? No answer was ever given.

The example of Pullman forces us to take a side. Either we accept the existence of unaccountable power in both towns and workplaces, or we demand that power be democratically accountable in both. In the words of Robert Dahl, a leading democratic theorist of the last fifty years, "*if* democracy is justified in governing the state, then it must *also* be justified in governing economic enterprises; and to say that it is *not* justified in governing economic enterprises is to imply that it is *not* justified in governing the state."[27]

If we believe in democracy, we believe that all power and authority between human beings needs to be accountable and that people should have a say in the major decisions that affect their lives. We should find the lack of democracy at work deeply troubling. We should insist that people have the choice of a democratic alternative to hierarchical work.

In capitalist society, most of us will spend more time in the workplace than anywhere else, with the possible exception of in our families. And yet these institutions, so central to our lives, remain characterized by exploitation and domination. It's instructive to recall that we live in an economic order where the richest corporation in the world, Apple, finds it necessary to install nets under the factory windows to reduce suicide attempts from its workers.[28] There has to be another way.

3

REALITIES OF CAPITALISM II

CONSUMERISM, GLOBALIZATION, AND ENVIRONMENTAL DESTRUCTION

T HE PIG, the ultimate symbol of voraciousness and gluttony, can consume four kilograms of food every day. Whereas contemporary Americans consume eighty-eight kilograms of resources per person every day—twenty-two times more.[1]

In the last seventy years the rich countries have engaged in the largest consumer binge in the history of our species. If everyone in the world were to live like an American, we would need five planets. We are not only consuming more than humans ever have, we are consuming more and more each year. The average American today spends 20 percent more than in 1990 (in real, inflation-adjusted terms) on cars, housing, and food; 80 percent more on clothes; and 300 percent more on furniture and household goods.[2]

Nothing epitomizes our consumption addiction better than the clothing industry. Even though masses of good clothes are available for everyone and thrift stores overflow with perfectly decent things, most of us, fuelled by billboards and fashion magazines, feel a need to constantly buy the latest trends. In 2007, the average American purchased a new piece of clothing every 5.4 days (67 new items every year), most of which would end up in mountains of garbage or overflowing the charity shops.[3] We are on a spiral of ever-growing consumption.

The standard capitalist myth is that the system simply responds to what people want. If people are greedy, so the story goes, that's their own problem. It's not the fault of the economic system.

The truth, however, is very different. For capitalism to function smoothly, the system requires consumer demand to stay strong. If people stop shopping, profits dip, workers are laid off, and the whole economy starts to falter. That's why in the weeks that followed the 9/11 attacks, President George W. Bush's main message to the public was *go shop!*[4] This is a profound paradox: for capitalism to function well, people need to feel inadequate. The system can only create jobs by producing an underlying unhappiness about not having enough.

CONSUMERISM: A SPIRAL OF DESIRE

How does the richest country in the history of humanity persuade its citizens that they are far too poor? That they should be continually dissatisfied with the things they have so that they'll be eager to buy new ones? The answer is that capitalism doesn't just respond to desires, it creates them.

Businesses in the United States today spend over $140 billion every year on advertising. That's more than the total amount the government spends on welfare ($135 billion). The *Harvard Business Review* interviewed chairpeople of large companies and found that 90 percent of them believe that it is impossible to sell a new product without an advertising campaign. The Jesuit religious order used to say, "Give me a child until he is seven and I will give you the man." Well, by the age of seven the typical American child has been exposed to roughly 630,000 ads. So it's not a huge surprise when they grow up to find pleasure in shopping and feel at home in the mall. Today, 93 percent of teenage girls in the United States say that shopping is their favourite activity.[5]

"Consumption"—a word that a hundred years ago meant destroy, use up, or waste—has become a central goal of our societies. And adults have even more reason to embrace consumerism, beyond the pangs of jealousy we feel when a friend has a newer computer or nicer clothes. For many people, our working lives are dreary and unrewarding. We can only get through the workday by consoling ourselves with the amount of money we're getting and fantasizing about how we'll spend it. In other words, consumerism is fuelled not just by crass materialism, but also by the sense that it compensates us for the alienation we feel from dehumanized work. This is one of the ways in which the problems of capitalism are intertwined. The hierarchical workplace feeds consumerism.

Consumerism is now such a deeply rooted part of our culture that it's often difficult to step outside of it to see how strong it really is. One antidote is spending time in poorer countries, where people have much less stuff but are often just as happy (if not more so). Another is studying history.

A thousand years ago, we would have thought that a steady supply of food and water, shelter, and heat constituted great wealth. A hundred years ago, Virginia Woolf was adamant that an income of £500 per year (enough for a room of one's own, food, clothing, shelter, plumbing with hot and cold water, and basic comforts) was all the money required to live a perfectly happy life. By the 1950s, most people in the West had far more than those basics—a house, a car, a fully stocked fridge, and a host of appliances—and yet still they wanted more. Today, the average suburban family has a much bigger house with several bedrooms and closets filled with clothes, two cars, and a garage filled with junk. Yet irrespective of the tremendous increase in wealth, the drive for more continues with no end in sight, indeed with no end even imaginable.

Most cultures experience greed, but no other culture has celebrated it as a virtue. No other culture has considered the accumulation of goods and wealth to be the essence of a good human life.

So one of the most radically anti-capitalist questions anyone can ask is: How much is enough?

At what point do we get off the hamster wheel? At what point do we say, I don't actually need that bigger apartment or those newer clothes. And I definitely don't want to sacrifice my dreams and free time by getting a corporate job to afford it. This is a question we must all try to consciously answer for ourselves. Otherwise, we will be led by the advertisers, the cultural priests of our time, to their preferred answer: There is never enough; the road to freedom and happiness is paved with more, more, and more …

There are good reasons for thinking that our current levels of consumption are far too high. The most pressing reason is that they are unsustainable. We are on a disastrous collision course with the environment. As Canadian environmentalist David Suzuki puts it, it is as if we were in a giant car driving full-speed ahead toward a brick wall, while the passengers are arguing about where they get to sit.[6]

Second, consumerism can seriously undermine our freedom, especially free time. Free time is important not just because it is enjoyable to relax after a long day at work. Rather, it is necessary for practically all our projects and goals in life. Our hopes and dreams may revolve around having a family, achieving excellence in music or art, contributing to the community, fighting for social justice, becoming an expert in a particular sport or activity, or having a rich social life. Whatever our aims are, they all require time free from work to pursue them.

Free time allows us to develop our lives in the directions we choose. The ancient Greek philosopher Aristotle insisted that the only purpose of work was to provide the basis for the leisure to pursue the important things in life.[7] Consumerism undermines this freedom. It chains us to a never-ending cycle of working and spending in which the only way we can keep buying more is by working harder and harder.

Consider this: from the 1950s to the 1990s, average U.S. productivity doubled. Society as a whole became twice as rich, so it had two basic choices about how to use its new wealth. People could take more time off. They could have said, *Let's stay where we are, at 1950s levels of consumption. Most everyone has their basic needs met—food, clothes, house, car, electricity, plumbing—and lots of their desires. So let's use our productivity increases as increased leisure. In that case, we could all work twenty hours a week, or work six months per year with six months off.*

The other option was to take the higher productivity as higher wages so that we could consume more. What did the U.S. population actually choose? None of the productivity increase went to increased leisure. In fact, by the 1990s the average American was working more hours than forty years earlier. All of the gains went to fuel increased consumption. In other words, society collectively chose to give up free time and environmental sustainability to be able to consume more things than no one really needs.[8] In the words of the famous philosopher Bertrand Russell, "can anything more insane be imagined?"[9]

Of course, in our societies, some people have more power than others to make such choices. But as a whole it's important to ask why the United States has chosen so much consumption over leisure (compared to other countries like Denmark and the Netherlands, who work far less)? There are two factors at play. The first and probably more important factor is that U.S. businesses have substantial incentives to prefer longer hours to shorter ones. It is generally more profitable for a business to hire one worker for 40 hours than two workers for 20 hours due to the difficulty of finding new skilled workers, the costs of training them, and the structure of benefit systems. (If a business has to make pension payments per person, instead of per hour, then it is cheaper for them to hire fewer workers and make hours longer). In Europe, businesses have the same incentives, but unions are often strong enough to resist them, and so able to push for shorter hours. The second factor is that of personal choice. Some populations have stronger consumerist cultures than others. The evidence shows that average Americans tend to be substantially more motivated by consumerism than most other countries.[10]

Astronomical levels of consumption might be justified if they were making us astronomically happy. Yet that is clearly not the case. A consumption-crazed society has not led to greater happiness. The more hours we spend looking through magazines, watching TV shows of the rich and famous, seeing thousands of ads plastered in every nook and cranny of the city, the easier it is to become unsatisfied with what we've got. The more we focus on consumption, the more sensitive we become to the things we don't have and therefore feel are lacking from our lives.

Over the last several decades, a new field of research has developed in economics—the economics of happiness. It analyzes the factors that make different societies more or less happy.[11] Standard practice is for individuals to be surveyed as to how happy they consider themselves (the technical term for this is "subjective well-being," or SWB). The most startling conclusion of the empirical research, demonstrated again and again, is that richer societies are not necessarily happier societies.

This is shown clearly in Figure 3.1, Happiness and Wealth. The average curve running through the middle of the graph shows the relationship between countries' wealth and well-being. Initially the curve rises steadily, as average happiness increases in tandem with increased wealth. This shows that money is important for happiness at low levels. When countries are poor, more income does indeed correlate with higher happiness.

However, once a modest degree of wealth is reached, the curve flattens out. Once a country gets rich enough that everyone can provide for their basic needs, more money provides almost no additional happiness. When a country passes a GDP of about $20,000 per capita (about half the current income level of the United States and Canada), people's happiness remains largely unaffected by wealth.

This shows that once our basic needs are satisfied, money is not the key to happiness. Indeed, most studies show that things like family and friends, a safe community, fulfilling work, and personal freedoms are the most important ingredients for happiness.[12] The

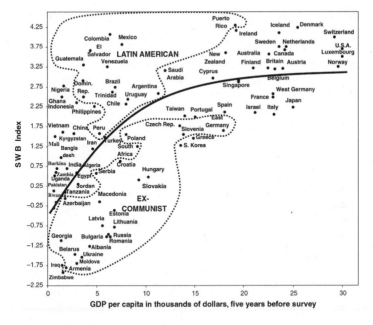

Figure 3.1. Happiness and Wealth

Source: R. Inglehart, R. Foa, C. Peterson, and C. Welzel, "Development, Freedom, and Rising Happiness: A Global Perspective (1981–2007)," *Perspectives on Psychological Science 3.4* (2008), 269.

experience of Japan illustrates this well. In the years 1958 to 1991, it experienced a tremendous six-fold increase in per person income, yet failed to experience any increase in the population's overall happiness.[13]

One eye-opening study examined the happiness levels of lottery winners. The researchers found that although winning the lottery made people happy for a short period of time, after about a year they were no happier than a control group of regular people (nor were they happier than they had been before winning).[14] People adapt to their circumstances, which is an important reason why consumption is likely to bring only short-lived happiness.

Additionally, most of us measure our happiness largely in relational terms—how well we are doing compared to the people around us. So in societies like Canada or the United States, which are very rich but also very unequal, the huge gap between average people and the wealthiest breeds dissatisfaction with yourself and pressure to keep up with Joneses. Richard Wilkinson and Kate Pickett, international experts on the effects of inequality in society, point out that a far more effective way of increasing societal happiness would be to focus on achieving more equality rather than more simply more total wealth. That way, the Joneses won't be too far ahead of everyone else, making us feel inadequate. The evidence shows, then, that we cannot spend our way to happiness. It's ludicrous to devote our lives to moneymaking, especially if this pursuit comes at the expense of our free time or other more important activities.

In short, it is not true that capitalism simply produces what people want in a neutral way. Capitalism turns us into gluttons: it makes pigs of people. It puts us on a never-ending hamster wheel of consumption, where we are all running as fast as we can after the people ahead of us. We are working as hard as possible but never actually getting any happier.

There is nothing wrong with consumption per se. But there is something deeply wrong—indeed, pathological—about a society that puts consumption on a pedestal as the ultimate purpose of life. Wouldn't it be more rational to consume so that we can do other, more important things in life? Consumption for consumption's sake is the ideology of the cancer cell. It is not a way of life that we should be proud of.

CORPORATE GLOBALIZATION: THE RACE TO THE BOTTOM

In 1999, when I was seventeen and just starting to think about politics, the World Trade Organization gathered for its annual meeting in downtown Seattle. The WTO economists were apostles of free trade and globalization. For years they had been repeating a seductive story. Globalization makes it easier for companies to move anywhere in the world. It allows corporations from the Global North to move to the Global South—to India, China, Mexico, and so on—bringing new technology, capital, and good jobs. The cheaper labour allows goods to be produced at a lower cost and imported back to the North. Globalization thus brings good jobs for people in the South and cheap goods for people in the North. A win-win!

And yet, as the delegates were giving speeches about prosperity and patting each other on the back, it became hard to ignore the not-too-distant sound of breaking glass. Outside the conference, tens of thousands of protesters—unionists, environmental activists, anarchists, and everything in between—had gathered to denounce the WTO's vision. The protesters outside the meeting had a very different understanding of globalization than the suits and economists inside.

While they agreed that corporate globalization made it easier for companies to move around the world, they disagreed that this was good for anyone except those companies' owners and shareholders. The reality of globalization, they said, was that large corporations, such as Nike and Gap, used their increased ability to move as a weapon. Companies were approaching their workforces in Canada or the United States and demanding that the workers get rid of their unions, cut their wages, and slash their benefits—or the business would move to Mexico or China and they would be out of a job altogether. (In fact, the threat of globalization is an important factor in the fall of private-sector unionization rates in the United States from 18.5 percent in 1983 to just 9 percent in 2003.)[15]

Moreover, it wasn't simply a case of one job shutting down in the North and another one opening up in the South. It was a case of good jobs (with decent wages, union protections, health and safety regulations, and environmental protocols) being replaced with bad ones, typified by sweatshops. First, a company like Nike would approach the government of, say, the Philippines. Nike would promise to come and build a factory that would provide several thousand jobs. But in return they wanted reduced taxes, lessened environmental regulation, and most importantly, a promise to prevent unions from forming. At the same time, Nike would approach Bangladesh, telling the government there that the Philippines was willing to offer a tax holiday of one year and few regulations. Could they make a better offer? Nike would then do the same with the governments of China, India, and so on. The company would thereby force countries to compete against each other to offer fewer taxes, cheaper labour, and increasingly lax regulations, all in order to entice new investment. The protesters had an apt name for this process: the race to the bottom.

In her well-known book *No Logo*,[16] journalist and activist Naomi Klein shone a bright light on the hidden truth of globalization. She documented the areas where multinational corporations set up factories. For instance, she described the Cavite Export Processing Zone, a free trade zone ninety miles south of Manila in the Philippines, which is a 680-acre walled-in industrial area with over two hundred factories and fifty thousand workers. Each factory workshop is windowless, made of cheap plastic and aluminum. Inside, rows of young people, mostly women, hunch over their machines in silence where they work twelve-hour days. "The management is military-style, the supervisors are often abusive, the wages below subsistence and the work low-skill and tedious," Klein wrote.

Some employers keep bathrooms padlocked except for two fifteen-minute breaks. Seamstresses at one factory sewing garments for Gap, Guess, and Old Navy have to urinate in plastic bags under their machines. There are rules against talking too much, and the occasional man or woman who dares to try to unionize often turns up lying in the street, beaten and bloody. To emphasize that unions won't be tolerated, a large sign posted in a central intersection in the Zone reads in big, bold letters: DO NOT LISTEN TO AGITATORS AND TROUBLE MAKERS.

The workers live in shantytowns on the outskirts of the Zone, or in dormitories made from converted farmhouses where "some rooms . . . are really pigpens with roofs slapped on them." Workers are supposed to earn the minimum wage—$6 per day. But if investors feel this minimum is too hard on them, they can apply for a government waiver, so most workers end up earning even less. Multinational corporations can rent these factories for dirt cheap—less than one cent per square foot. Moreover any corporation that goes to the Cavite Zone is given a tax holiday, paying no income or property taxes for their first five years of operations.

So the race to the bottom pushes wages and conditions down for working people, and pushes profits up for corporations. On top of this, the profits rarely stay in the country for long. Instead, most of the profits are vacuumed back to rich executives and shareholders in the North. More often than not they end up in secret bank accounts in Switzerland or the Cayman Islands to avoid taxation in the North as well. Indeed, for all the talk of how good free trade is for the poor nations of the world, the central fact is that money continues to flow *out* of many poor countries toward the rich ones.

This is the truth of globalization: not prosperity for all, but fabulous wealth for a small minority and a race to the bottom for everyone else.

This is not to say that trade is a bad thing. It's important for poor countries to have access to rich markets in the Global North. But the goal should not be "free trade"—where corporate shareholders benefit at the expense of everyone else. It should be fair trade, where the gains of exchange are shared equitably.

When defenders of globalization hear this critique, they usually admit the facts. It's pretty hard to find people who disagree that good unionized jobs in the North are being replaced with sweatshop jobs in the South. But they try to excuse it in two ways. First, you often hear that sweatshops are better than nothing. And in a sense this is true—obviously *anything* is better than starvation. But why are those the only options? A sweatshop may be better than nothing, but it's just as clear that it's worse than a good job.

For example, if a child is getting bullied by a classmate in school who says "Give me your lunch money or I'll punch you," it makes sense for the child to give up the money. But it would be strange for the rest of us to simply shrug and say that the situation is okay, as we do with sweatshops, because it's better than the alternative. Any reasonable person would say, No, there must be other options; we need to get a teacher involved to stop the bullying. The same is true with sweatshops. We need to insist that starvation or sweatshops aren't the only options. Good jobs with decent regulation are also possible.

A second, more fundamental excuse for the situation is that it's simply impossible to ensure good jobs. Market competition means that any company willing to use sweatshops will inevitably drive under companies that aren't. In other words, the race to the bottom is the inevitable outcome of capitalist competition in a free market. People in the South have to work in sweatshops. People in the North have to start working longer for cheaper or they'll lose out. There's no point complaining about it, it's just the reality of how the market works.

This is wrong. Markets do not have to work like this. It's completely false that markets can only exist in one particular way and can never be changed. Markets are highly flexible and plastic things. They can and have been shaped very differently to allow different kinds of competition and produce very different results.

Consider the example of a typical clothing factory in England in the 1850s. Such factories were what we would now call sweatshops. Workers were often compelled to work twelve- to fourteen-hour days. Unions were illegal. About one-third of the workers were children.[17] There were no health and safety regulations, and definitely no environmental ones. So what happened when socialists and other activists started protesting these conditions?

We want a unionized factory, they said, with a ten-hour day, where no children are working, and with basic health and safety regulations. You can well imagine. The capitalists and their newspapers sneered. They called the socialists fools and declared that such workplaces were impossible and utopian—they would inevitably be driven under in the market competition against the regular sweatshop firms.

In a superficial sense they were right. It's true that the unionized firm was not going to succeed in a competition against the sweatshop firm in the kind of market system that existed in the 1850s. But in a deeper sense, they were fundamentally wrong. Competition is always structured by the rules of the market, and such rules can always be changed. We know this with certainty, because the unionized, anti-child-labour firm that was so obviously doomed to failure in the 1850s is today the standard. This is because activists struggling for generations have managed to change the rules of the market system, making child labour illegal and ensuring collective bargaining rights. Today the old sweatshop firm is no longer the most competitive—it's simply illegal.

And this lesson is true much more broadly. Ask yourself: Does the fact that pregnant women are less productive than men justify firing them so that their firms will be more competitive? No. Feminists are right to insist that we should not accept that kind of competition, but instead regulate the market to provide for maternity leave. Does the fact that polluting firms are cheaper than green firms mean we should allow green firms to be driven under by the competition? No. We should change the nature of market competition, for instance, by instituting a carbon tax.

So coming back to globalization, there is nothing at all inevitable about sweatshops. There is nothing inevitable about losing good jobs and replacing them with bad ones. We are not helpless against the forces of the market. Markets are constructed and regulated by the state, and so people in democratic states can insist that their markets be shaped differently. We can pass legislation to force companies to operate differently.

We therefore need to fight for the WTO and other such bodies to implement global labour standards, including the right to unionize, minimum wages, environmental standards, and limits on overtime. We need to ban sweatshops across the world. There is no reason why it is possible to have international trade agreements, but not international labour agreements. The question is not whether it's possible to rid sweatshops from the market—our own history proves that it is. The real question is whether we are willing to fight for it.

ENVIRONMENTAL DESTRUCTION

In May 2013, monitoring stations in Hawaii detected that the amount of carbon dioxide in the atmosphere had passed 400 parts per million (ppm). It was one more marker on our march to environmental madness. Scientists across the world agree that 350 ppm is a safe level, which means that we are quickly entering very dangerous and unchartered territory. When was the last time that human beings had experienced 400 ppm? The answer is scary: never. Not once in the span of human history have carbon levels been this high. The earth itself has not experienced this level of carbon in the atmosphere since the Pliocene age, three million years ago.

The science of global warming is now all but incontrovertible. The burning of fossil fuels since the Industrial Revolution in the 1800s has caused an explosion in emissions of carbon dioxide and other greenhouse gases that lock heat into the earth's atmosphere. The latest report from the Intergovernmental Panel on Climate Change states that unless global carbon emissions are reduced 21 to 61 percent below the 1990 baseline level by 2050 (and a near 100 percent reduction by 2100) carbon levels will inevitably reach 450 ppm, which will cause at least a two-degree rise in temperatures.[18] A two-degree rise is the threshold at which major ecosystems are expected to collapse, forever changing basic environmental and weather conditions, and potentially bringing catastrophic climate changes. But not only are we not close to reaching this target for reductions, we are actually moving in the wrong direction. Since 1990 we have actually had a 31 percent increase in emissions.[19]

Although these statistics are very scary, some people have a mild reaction to climate change. *So it gets two degrees warmer. Big deal. This country is too cold as it is!* In fact it's a huge deal. If temperatures rise two degrees, it's likely that more than two billion people will face water shortages. The lush interior of the Amazon basin will become void of vegetation. Mass flooding will devastate large coastal areas: a sea rise of one metre could permanently flood 21 percent of Bangladesh, de-housing 15 million people. Small island nations may disappear altogether. Large parts of Africa will be turned into desert. Vital rivers, such as the Ganges, will start to dry up. Flooding and famine will produce climate refugees in the hundreds of millions, causing mass political instability. Researchers are warning that climate change could kill 184 million people in Africa alone before the century is over. This is roughly double as many people as died in the First and Second World Wars combined.[20]

One standard retort is that none of this need worry us too much because capitalism, through the magic of the market, will spontaneously adapt to deal with any problems. When natural resources become rare, they will become more expensive, and so people will consume less of them.

But if capitalism were really able to develop an equilibrium with the natural world, we would not see thousands of animal species threatened with extinction, forests being felled, seas emptied, and lakes poisoned. Let's take a simple example. People want to eat tuna. So fishers search the ocean trying to profit from this demand. To maximize their profit, fishers trawl the waters with massive nets, disrupting natural ecologies and catching hundreds of other species that are killed and thrown back—26 percent of the world's catch is discarded annually.[21] Economists call such damages and wastes "externalities," which we'll discuss further below.

As tuna start to get overfished, the price goes up. This may make some fishers give up and look for different jobs, but it also makes successful catches more rewarding. So it gives the remaining fishers an incentive to find every last tuna before their competitor can, and to care less and less about the natural environment, such as the welfare of the dolphins caught in the nets. So fishers start competing against each other by going out earlier each morning, sailing further into the ocean, fishing deeper, and using larger nets that catch more of everything. In this way fishing stocks can be driven to extinction. Today, an incredible 90 percent of all the large fish in the ocean have been removed.[22] Capitalism is turning our oceans into watery deserts.

It's noteworthy that where fish stocks are being successfully maintained, this has usually occurred by adopting non-capitalist measures. For example, by using the state to regulate the amount of total fish that can be caught each year. Or combining competing fishers into a co-operative that democratically divides the total allowable catch.

Far from capitalism being intrinsically able to deal with environmental problems, it is more reasonable to believe the opposite. Capitalism is inherently environmentally destructive. There are two fundamental reasons why: capitalism is based on never-ending growth, and it has no incentive to care about the value of nature (this is the problem of externalities).

Never-Ending Growth

Neoliberal capitalism's typical dynamic is to grow without limits. And while the economy could theoretically grow forever, it is always contained within the larger environmental system that cannot. There are natural limits to what the environment can sustain, both in terms of how much is taken out and how much waste can be reabsorbed. Our economy is starting to push beyond those limits.

There are several motors for this never-ending growth.

- It is propelled by consumerism and the materialistic desire for more. Sixty billion tons of resources are now extracted from the earth every year—about 50 percent more than just thirty years ago. Corporations extract the equivalent of 112 Empire State Buildings in raw material every day, all to provide the latest toys and trends.[23]

- Continual growth helps alleviate the central tension between workers and bosses over who gets what. How do you deal with a situation where both workers and employers are fighting for a bigger slice of the pie? One way is to grow the pie. It's much easier to overlook the fact that the rich are getting twenty times richer if the poor are getting twice as rich as well. Harvard history professor Charles Maier puts it well: "The concept of growth as a surrogate for redistribution is the great conservative idea of the last generation."[24] Constantly increasing growth allows society to avoid the only other option—that present wealth needs to be shared.

- The last motor that pushes growth is the logic of competition itself. Capitalism needs to grow for the system to be stable. Every business is pressured by the competition to grow or die. Capitalism's internal mechanics are like those of a bicycle. A bicycle is stable only when it is moving forward; capitalism is relatively stable when it's growing at a couple of percent per year. Unfortunately, perpetual growth is destroying the environment. Since the 1960s, global emissions have increased every year, except in devastating recessions (in the mid-1970s, early 1980s, and 2009). So the only time the environment is not being degraded is when the economy is in crisis. In other words, capitalist economic stability and environmental sustainability are contradictory goals. Within the parameters of neoliberal capitalism, you can only have one of these outcomes.

For all of these reasons—consumerism, softening class conflict, and competitive pressure—capitalism's inherent drive to expand puts it on a collision course with the environment. It's possible to imagine a "delinking" of the economy from the use of natural resources, for instance by inventing new green technologies. But the evidence suggests that technology alone is extremely unlikely to save us.[25] We should try to delink as much as possible. But dramatic reductions are needed in the production and consumption of fossil fuels right now. Economist and philosopher Kenneth Boulding sums up the situation well: "Only a madman or an economist could believe that exponential growth can go on forever in a finite world."[26]

The Cost of Externalities

Capitalism is also inherently damaging to the environment because of what economists call "externalities." These are costs (or benefits) that apply to people other than the immediate buyer or seller. Let's say a factory produces TVs. In the course of production it emits a pollutant into a nearby river, which causes damage to the environment and makes people downriver sick. The resulting costs are externalities; the people being affected weren't part of the actual exchange so their desires aren't taken into account.

Because of externalities, the market price for goods and services does not reflect the true social costs. In this example, the factory is able to externalize the true costs of production onto other people—they don't have to pay sick people's hospital bills. Consumers, meanwhile, are offered artificially cheap TVs. They are encouraged to buy more than they would if they had to pay the true costs.

More than anything else, global warming is caused by externalities. The increasingly enormous costs of carbon pollution are simply ignored by the people who produce it. Our factories, energy companies, and airlines spew masses of carbon into the atmosphere, but they don't have to pay for doing so. The reason easyJet is able to sell flights for $100 all across Europe is because the true costs—the desertification in Africa, the sinking of Bangladesh, and so on—are excluded from the bill. But ignoring the costs doesn't mean that they don't exist. They're just externalized by the business onto other people—in this case, often poorer, browner people, living far away. Neither the producer nor the consumer has an incentive to care about these people. As long as carbon-emitting businesses are allowed to evade paying for the environmental damage they're causing, as long as they are allowed to skip out on the bill, they have every incentive to simply continue what they're doing. Burn, baby, burn.

In sum, capitalism is inherently unsustainable because of its insatiable drive to grow and its ability to ignore, or externalize, the real value of nature and the true cost of its destruction.

A SOCIETY GONE MAD

An alien from another planet looking at our civilization could hardly be blamed for concluding that our societies have gone mad. It has become normal to work long hours in alienating jobs for businesses that are destroying the planet, so that we can consume goods produced in sweatshops, which don't make us any happier. All this in order to keep up with people we don't know and emulate others we'll never meet.

The drives to consume and to maximize profits have pushed corporations to every corner of the globe in a race to the bottom that worsens working conditions and ravages the natural world. Seeing this, many people have suggested that humanity's relationship with the natural environment is parasitical, that of a virus or a cancer. But it's not people that are a virus. Indigenous communities rarely destroy their own ecosystems. And significant numbers of people in every country in the world would prefer to live more sustainably if they had the power to do so.

Humanity is not the problem. The virus is our economic system; the cancer is capitalism.

4

SHORT-TERM
ALTERNATIVES

REBUILDING
SOCIAL DEMOCRACY

IMAGINE if Americans woke up tomorrow and decided to try something new. They would redistribute some of the income of the top 1 percent of households, so that the highest income would be one million dollars per year. This tax would not affect 99 percent of the population at all. The other 1 percent would remain very, very rich. Nevertheless, the tax would raise enough revenue to provide free university tuition, universal preschool, year-long paid maternity leave, and a 75 percent increase of welfare rates. There would also be enough left to achieve the United Nations' Millennium Development Goals (eradicating extreme poverty and hunger and providing universal primary education across the globe).[1]

In this chapter, we'll explore some policies that already exist outside of North America. The most powerful way to puncture the myth that there is no alternative is to recognize that many alternatives already do exist. In addition, I want to show that it's possible to do more than simply change a couple of policies here and there. It's possible to have a fundamentally different kind of system. This is the example of social democracy, particularly as it exists in the Nordic countries of Sweden, Norway, Finland, and Denmark.

Nordic social democracy is by no means perfect, and in the next chapter we'll look at ways to improve it. But as an initial step, it is an excellent alternative to neoliberal capitalism.

INEQUALITY

Are there alternatives to the massive wealth inequality that we currently see in Canada, the United Kingdom, Ireland, Australia, New Zealand, and the United States? Absolutely. We can see this even in our own histories.

From President Roosevelt's New Deal in the 1930s to the Second World War, the United States enacted policies that drastically reduced inequality. During the war, top income tax rates were at 90 percent, and they stayed high for thirty years. When President Reagan entered office in 1981, the highest tax rate was still 75 percent. By the time he left in 1989 it was 33 percent.[2] Moreover, the legal environment after the New Deal made it easier to form unions, which were instrumental in reducing inequality. In 1954, 34 percent of U.S. workers belonged to unions. Today 11 percent do. It's estimated that the decline in union density in the 1980s by itself explains about 20 percent of the rise in wage inequality.[3]

Today, the Nordic states consistently place among the most egalitarian countries in the world. Whereas in the United States, the average CEO makes 200 times the salary of the average worker, in Sweden it's 15 times.[4] In the United States, 12 percent of the population is poor (that is, living off less than 40 percent of the median household income). In Norway only 1.7 percent is poor. The U.S. welfare system (with its pitifully small welfare cheques, food stamps, and pensions) brings 44 percent of poor people out of poverty, while the Danish system brings out 85 percent.

How much are countries able to reduce their inequality by using taxes and redistribution? While the United States achieves only a 17 percent reduction of inequality, Sweden achieves a 37 percent reduction. The neoliberal countries as a whole reduce inequality by 23 percent, whereas the Nordic countries reduce it by 33 percent.[5]

Scholars of comparative political economy point to three main mechanisms through which the Nordic states have reduced inequality: strong unions, a strong welfare state, and government policies of full employment.

Strong Unions

First, Nordic countries have high levels of union membership. For instance, in Sweden 70 percent of the working population is unionized, compared to 11 percent in the United States.[6] Unions provide workers with the strength to bargain collectively, so that more of the profits from businesses go to workers instead of to their bosses. Unionization also allows for co-ordinated bargaining across industries and across the economy as a whole.

In Sweden—and to a lesser degree in other Nordic countries— co-ordinated union bargaining has allowed unions to pursue "sol- idaristic" wage policies. Unions bargain to raise the wages of the lowest earners, while simultaneously volunteering to limit the earnings of the highest. This has two important effects: it reduces inequality and it makes the whole economy more efficient. Wage compression squeezes the profits of less-efficient firms, driving them out of business. Simultaneously, it restrains the wages of high- paid workers in more-efficient firms, allowing the firms to expand.

More generally, unions provide the backbone for progressive social and political movements to reshape society. The stronger the unions, the stronger the progressive forces of the country. And the more likely the country is to get any kind of progressive reform.

A Strong Welfare State

Nordic countries have generous welfare systems that provide high-quality, universally accessible services. These services include public health care, free education (for example, in addition to providing regular schooling, Sweden provides free daycare for all toddlers, as well as free university), welfare and retraining pro- grams, good pensions, and generous parental leave.

The Nordic system is funded by progressive taxation in which the rich pay a much higher rate than the poor. This is doubly effective for reducing inequality: the welfare system raises up the bottom, while progressive taxation lowers the top. Total tax revenue in 2013 was 47.6 percent of gross domestic product in Denmark—almost double the U.S. amount of 25.4 percent.[7]

While income tax in the U.S. is still progressive, overall the tax system has become regressive. Billionaire Warren Buffett pays about 17 percent tax (because most of his income comes from investments, not from wages like most people), whereas his secretary pays 36 percent.[8]

Progressive taxation has been a reliable method of reducing inequality, especially in the twentieth century. But some new tax ideas are gaining interest recently. One is a significant property or land value tax.

Rich people, particularly in big cities, own parcels of land that over the years have exploded in value simply because they are located in desirable places. Indeed, properties in London have become so valuable that simply owning a house will make you more money than going out and working. The average house increases in value £500 a day. That means property owners will make more in two days than an average worker will make in a week.[9] The most expensive flat in central London is worth £135 million, yet the owner paid only £1,369 in property tax in 2012, or 0.001 percent of its value.[10] Note that the land hasn't become more valuable due to anything the owners contributed. The land has increased in value because it's located in a thriving, vibrant city where many people want to live. In other words, the increased value of the land is caused by us. It's a result of our cities being desirable places to live, because of transport systems, schools, culture, and so on.

Since we as a society are responsible for this new wealth, we have an obvious right to levy a tax on it. If this tax were made proportional, properties that are worth more would be charged a higher rate. Such a tax would create more equality and raise significant revenues to fund public services.

Shutting Down the Tax Havens

Taxation is only useful in reducing inequality and funding the welfare state when the rich are forced to pay it. Unfortunately, there has been an explosion of tax dodging in recent years. A tax haven is a place, like the Bahamas, Switzerland, or the Cayman Islands, where wealth can be held secretly and with little or no taxation. In 2008, the U.S. Government Accountability Office estimated that 83 of the country's 100 biggest companies had subsidiaries in tax havens. Overall, it is estimated that about a quarter of total global wealth is held in tax havens.

Corporations use tax havens by setting up different locations of their business in different parts of the world. By setting up shop in tax havens, they are able to declare less profits in countries where there are high taxes while declaring more profits in tax havens where there are low taxes. So a banana company might open up a subsidiary in the Cayman Islands, then claim that all of its profits were made there, and so avoid paying taxes in the places where the bananas were actually grown and sold. This is not a make-believe example. In 2006, the *Guardian* newspaper found that the world's three biggest banana companies did nearly $750 million of business in Britain while paying only $235,000 in taxes. That's a tax rate of 0.031 percent, a thousand times less than normal working people pay.

A major goal of any progressive movement must be to shut down these tax havens as soon as possible.*

* All statistics from Nicholas Shaxson, *Treasure Islands: Tax Havens and the Men Who Stole the World* (London: The Bodley Head, 2011).

Full Employment

Finally, Nordic countries have reduced inequality by pursuing full employment. The wealth of the people at the bottom of the spectrum is best improved by ensuring that they can get steady work.

From the 1950s to the 1980s, the Nordic countries managed to keep unemployment below 3 percent. At that level, pretty much everyone who wanted a job could get one. (Unemployment worsened in the 1990s, and recovered somewhat in the 2000s.) To maintain full employment, Nordic countries used two government tools. They used monetary policy, keeping interest rates low. With low interest, it's easier for businesses to borrow money to expand and hire new workers. And they used fiscal policy, or direct government spending. Spending on schools, hospitals, infrastructure, and so on means hiring more people.

This spending has a positive social impact beyond job growth. To take just one example, Nordic countries spend 6.2 percent of their GDP on public education, compared to the neoliberal average of 4.8 percent.[11] This investment creates good, reliable jobs for teachers. It also leads the Nordic countries to have the highest average literacy scores in the world, and the most equal spread of test scores.[12]

EXPLOITATION AND DOMINATION IN THE WORKPLACE

In capitalist societies, as we have seen, bosses tend to have substantial power over their workers. When this power is not checked, bosses demand more time, effort, and obedience while paying less in return. Workplaces can become sweatshops and oppressive hierarchies. Over the last 150 years, three main methods have been developed to limit the power of the bosses and expand workers' freedom: unionization, regulation, and co-determination.

Unionization

Without unions we wouldn't have a minimum wage, a forty-hour working week, old age pensions, or a universal health care system. We wouldn't even have a weekend! A union is the basic counterweight to the power of the employer. So it's no accident that the countries where workers have the most freedom—the most ability to influence their schedules, vacations, pensions, wages, and other conditions—are precisely those countries, such as Sweden and France, with high levels of union coverage.

You might wonder if I'm being too uncritical of unions. Don't unionized workers become lazy and unproductive because it's impossible for employers to fire them? It's important to recognize the conflicting points of view here. Since employers make more money the harder workers work, any work that is done at less than full speed will seem to them to be lazy.

A woman wants to take time off for maternity. A father wants to leave work at 3 p.m. to pick up his child from school. A worker wants to work part-time so she can volunteer at a soup kitchen. A disabled worker gets tired easily and needs to take multiple breaks. From the bosses' perspective, these are all unproductive. What appears to the employer as unproductive appears to the worker as security. So whenever you hear that unions make workers lazy, step back and ask: Why should we take the bosses' perspective? Shouldn't our default position be that it's better for workers to be protected than to be exploited?

We can agree that it's good for workers to be motivated to produce high-quality work. But the question is, What's the best way to do this? One way is to give employers lots of power in order to motivate workers through negative incentives of fear: *Do what I say or else!* But this isn't the only way. The alternative is to motivate workers through positive incentives. For example, through profit sharing, shared decision-making at work, partnership, and a sense of responsibility and pride. The point of unions isn't to demotivate, but to force employers to rely less on negative incentives and more on positive ones. It is to move away from dehumanizing fear and toward humanizing empowerment.

Of course, unions can and do fail at their tasks. They can fail to soften negative incentives, and they can fail to create positive ones. They can fail to protect workers who genuinely need protection, while spending too much time and resources protecting the jobs of jerks who come to work drunk or sexually harass their colleagues. Unions can fall into the rut of providing insurance for individual workers, instead of struggling to reform society for the good of us all. They can be internally corrupt and undemocratic.

But that doesn't diminish the fact that the essence of unions is an incredibly important thing. It is to protect working people and struggle for a more egalitarian society. When a certain union is acting badly, it's important to get involved to make it better. Progressive people shouldn't feel a need to defend every union, regardless of its record.

But we should be clear that good unions are exceptionally important. And we should never forget that most of the criticism levelled at unions, particularly by the right-wing media, is not honest criticism. It is not meant to improve unions, but to discredit them so that bosses become more powerful and workers become weaker.

Regulation

Progressive movements have also fought for regulation to reduce workplace hierarchy. Regulations are legal boundaries to what employers are allowed to do. For example, regulations oblige employers to negotiate with unions, to implement basic health and safety protocols, and to not discriminate against workers' race or gender.

Beyond these basics, many alternative regulations can further reduce workplace hierarchy. Employers can be made to increase their scheduling transparency so that workers know their schedules at least two weeks ahead. That allows them to plan their lives more regularly. We need regulations giving workers more control over their hours, such as increased vacation time or increased flexibility (sometimes called "flextime"). There are important examples of this in the Netherlands, which we'll look at below.

Parental leave is another vital regulation. Mothers should be allowed to take significant time off to have a child without fear of losing their job. Men and adoptive parents likewise need strong paternity regulations so that caregiving responsibilities, as well as the joys of parenthood, can be shared between partners.

Most advanced countries offer some parental leave. But it's often far too short and there is little flexibility in allowing parents to return to work slowly in order to balance work and family life. Only four countries in the world do not guarantee women some form of paid maternity leave: Papua New Guinea, Swaziland, Liberia, and the United States. In the United States, mothers receive only twelve weeks of unpaid leave and no paid leave.[13]

The Swedish alternative is much better. There the state guarantees sixteen months of paid parental leave, paid at 80 percent of one's income. It may be shared between the partners in any way that they wish, as long as the minority caregiver (usually the father) takes at least two months of this time. This policy has been very successful in motivating fathers to take time off. This in turn has led to more gender balance in caregiving, and so has reduced discrimination faced by women in getting jobs, raises, and promotions.[14]

Co-determination

The most ambitious regulations go beyond requiring employers to negotiate with the workers. Policies of shared governance, usually called "co-determination," require employers to share decision-making with the workers. Co-determination exists in Sweden, Denmark, Norway, Austria, Luxembourg, and Germany. It requires that a number of seats on the boards of directors of large firms be reserved for worker representatives.

The practice has gone the furthest in Germany, where the Co-determination Act of 1976 provides worker representation on the supervisory board of all large firms. (The supervisory board elects the management board, which controls the firm's day-to-day operations). The Act provides workers with one-third of the representatives on the board for firms of 501 to 1,000 workers, and just under one-half for firms larger than 2,000 workers, with shareholders getting the other half (and the tie-breaker vote).[15]

So instead of the usual model where employers make decisions and unions react, co-determination requires employers and union representatives to make at least some decisions jointly. In this way co-determination starts to challenge the deep structures of workplace hierarchy. It provides workers with enhanced say over their working lives.

CONSUMERISM

To combat consumerism, we need to find ways to shift away from a *high-spending* society, based on working more in order to shop more. We need instead to build a *high-leisure* society. One that works and shops less and places more value on free time. This is going to require dramatic shifts in how our economies work, as well as shifts in our cultural values.

Economic Changes

To begin, we need to decrease work hours. One way is simply to legislate a reduced workweek. For example, since 2000, France has had a standard thirty-five-hour workweek, after which hours must be counted as overtime. Moreover, in most European countries, you get at least four weeks of paid vacation time.

Another way is to increase workers' control over their schedules. Unfortunately, in the neoliberal countries, flexibility is moving in the wrong direction. In Britain, for instance, 19 percent of workers in hotels and restaurants are now on "zero-hour" contracts. These workers receive zero hours of guaranteed work, and instead are perpetually on call for whenever the boss summons them.[16] This provides wonderful flexibility for employers but total insecurity for workers.

We should be fighting for the opposite: flexibility for workers to choose their hours. The best current example is in the Netherlands. The Working Hours Adjustment Act of 2000 gives all workers the right to adjust their hours, upwards or downwards. An employer can only refuse if they can prove that such a switch would result in serious financial hardship for the firm.

Such economic changes often lead to corresponding cultural changes. People become accustomed to the reduced hours, and start to enjoy them much more than they thought they would. For example, when Bell Canada asked Canadian technicians if they would accept an 8 percent pay cut for correspondingly fewer hours, 90 percent said no. They wanted the money, not the time. But the company did it anyway. Four months after the policy had been implemented, workers' preferences had shifted remarkably. Only 15 percent wanted to return to full-time work.[17]

Cultural Changes

For such economic changes to develop, people must start to doubt that the key to happiness is being able to buy newer and better stuff. Policies can help—such as fighting for ad-free spaces, particularly on children's TV and in public places like schools, parks, community centres, and public transit. But culture only really changes when people start talking about things differently.

In our conversations with family, friends, and colleagues, in classrooms, workplaces, bars, and living rooms, and in all kinds of different media from newspapers and radios to blogs and tweets, we need to be more critical of consumerism. We need to challenge the idea that a forty-hour workweek is a necessary way to live, and sing the praises of free time. We need to express disappointment when materially secure people choose more work over more free time, and express outrage when others don't even have this choice. We need to raise our eyebrows when people congratulate themselves on buying the latest brand item, scoff when they congratulate themselves on being workaholics, and shake our heads when fathers don't take time off to be with their kids.

We need to ask why when our friends tell us they couldn't possibly be happy without owning a house, and express incredulity when middle-class individuals can't imagine living on $40,000 a year (far richer than the vast majority of human beings are now or have ever been). It's helpful to remember that many, if not all, of the great cultures of world history had an ideal of a good life that was not focused on accumulating money.[18] Although it feels normal for us, from a historical perspective, our culture is a strange one.

Perhaps most important is to envision and articulate a different kind of life. One where people work less, buy less, and spend more time developing their passions. We might spend our time building relationships, cooking with friends, or gardening at home. We might play sports or music, care for our neighbours, or get involved in the community. This would be a life of smaller TVs but stronger community ties; a life of less money, but more freedom and happiness.

We need to paint a picture where the important things in life get better and better, but the amount of money required—the size of our home and amount of possessions—stays relatively constant. Then we can feel that this is all we need for a good life. And we can pronounce those radically anti-capitalist words: *Enough is enough.*

CORPORATE GLOBALIZATION

It's not globalization per se that's a problem. As Keynes once said, "Ideas, knowledge, science, hospitality, travel—these are the things which should of their nature be international."[19] But what should not be globalized is corporate power. The main alternative to corporate globalization is human-centred globalization. This approach focuses not simply on GDP growth but on sustainable development and good jobs for all.

How can we protect good jobs in the Global North? We already mentioned the most important things—unionization, regulation, and where possible, co-determination. We can also impose taxes

Social Protectionism

Philosopher and economist David Schweickart has an ambitious idea for improving global standards. He calls it "socialist protectionism."

A tariff should be imposed on goods imported from poor countries into Northern countries. This tariff would protect workers in the North from low-wage or environmentally unfriendly competition. At the same time, the money collected from the tariffs would be sent back to the country where the goods originated, to agencies that are likely to be effective at alleviating poverty. These would be state agencies in some cases, and in others, unions, environmental groups, women's groups, or non-governmental organizations.

Such a system would simultaneously protect good jobs in the North and help to alleviate dire poverty in the South.*

* David Schweickart, *After Capitalism* (Lanham, Maryland: Rowman & Littlefield, 2002), 82.

on products from the Global South that are made artificially cheap by exploiting the workforce or the environment. A tax on such goods levels the playing field. Dirty companies shouldn't drive under better, more socially conscious companies, particularly unionized or co-operative workplaces.

In the Global South, good jobs can be protected by fair trade practices. That way, consumers in the North support good jobs. The flip side is exerting pressure against bad jobs through consumer boycotts. Boycotts can be successful in significantly changing corporate practices. They work best when they are led by the workers directly affected by the companies' bad practices. In the 1990s, there was an anti-sweatshop boycott against Nike; in 2014,

SodaStream's production in the occupied Palestinian territories was targeted. For recent examples of successful boycotts, see the Ethical Consumer website (ethicalconsumer.org).

Finally, we need to fight for the World Trade Organization and other such bodies to implement global labour standards. These standards would include the right to unionize, minimum wages, environmental regulations, limits on overtime, and so on.

ENVIRONMENTAL DESTRUCTION

The scale of our environmental problems is alarming. But there are many proposals out there for reducing our environmental impact. The biggest problem is not that we don't know what to do, but that there is so little will to do it.

Natural Resource Depletion

Environmentalists have long advocated for regulations to set strict limits on the amount of resources that can be extracted, burned, or harvested each year. These limits cannot be set according to what businesses want, since they will set the limits far too high. They must instead defer to what scientists say is required for ecological sustainability.

With political will, it is easy enough to limit natural resource depletion. For example, a fishing limit set on lobster in New Zealand led to a five-fold increase in their number in five years.[20] Conservation zones in countries around the world have proven essential for protecting biodiversity.

Externalities

We need to put a price on the costs of production that are externalized onto people who are neither the buyer nor seller. Companies should be forced to pay the true costs of their production—they can't just leave the planet with the bill. Two mechanisms for doing this are putting a tax on the externality or using a system of cap-and-trade.

Cap-and-Trade vs. Tax

There is some debate about whether taxation or cap-and-trade is a better approach to externalities. Radical economist Robin Hahnel, for example, argues that while a tax might be theoretically preferable, we are more likely to get good practical results from a cap-and-trade system.* When the issue is a tax, the experts are the (usually conservative) economists. But when the issue is a cap, the experts are the (often more progressive) scientists.

Although the U.S. cap-and-trade approach to acid rain was a success, these systems can be easily undermined. The European Union Emissions Trading Scheme, for example, has been a spectacular failure. The caps were set far too low, in order to appease business groups instead of reflecting scientific evidence. This meant that carbon remained so cheap that it didn't actually change businesses' behaviour. The only thing it seems to have done is create a new group of wealthy financiers engaged in emissions trading.

* Robin Hahnel, "Why Cap and Trade and Not a Carbon Tax?," Z Communications, www.zcomm.org, Feb. 25, 2010.

A successful cap-and-trade program was initiated by the United States in 1990 to deal with acid rain. Coal companies were producing a large amount of damaging sulphur emissions, which mixed with rainfall forming in the atmosphere. These emissions were externalities—they imposed huge costs on the environment, but the companies didn't pay for them. The program set a cap—based on what the scientists said was necessary—on the total amount of sulphur that was allowed to be produced in a year. This maximum was then divided into quotas that gave each company the right to produce that amount of sulphur emissions. Each year the cap was reduced bit by bit, and companies that went over their quotas were heavily fined. This forced them to adjust their practices.

In addition, companies were free to trade their quotas. Now emissions had a price; they were worth something. Companies thereby acquired a powerful incentive to reduce emissions. The more environmentally friendly they could make their factories, the less of their quota they would need to use. They could then sell the leftover amount to other firms for profit.

By 2009, sulphur emissions had successfully been reduced to 67 percent below 1980 levels—an even better reduction than was being aimed for. Consequently, the amount of acidic sulphur returning to earth has dropped by roughly 50 percent across the eastern United States.[21]

Global Warming

Global warming can't be solved by individual countries acting alone. We need a global agreement. If everyone isn't involved, there are enormous incentives to "free ride"—to be dirtier than the country beside you, in order to steal their business out from under them. Fortunately, we already have the framework of an international agreement in the form of the Kyoto Protocol. One hundred ninety-two states signed up for it in 1997: every country in the world except Andorra, South Sudan, and, disgustingly, the United States and Canada. (These countries finally joined the consensus and signed the Paris Agreement in 2016.)

Environmental activists have been clear for years that two things are required to enable an international framework to prevent global environmental catastrophe. The first is a global cap on emissions based on the science. This cap needs to be legally binding—it can't just be an airy-fairy number that countries can ignore without any repercussions. There have to be real, punitive consequences, such as high fines, for failing to meet the target.

Second, the framework needs to recognize that different countries have different amounts of responsibility for global warming,

The Greenhouse Development Rights Framework

The Greenhouse Development Rights (GDR) framework is one innovative proposal for dealing with global warming in a just manner. The idea is that the obligation of different countries to respond to climate change depends on two factors. The first is a country's *responsibility* for causing global warming—its climate debt. The second is its capacity for fixing it, with the assumption that people below a poverty threshold have a primary right to development and so rightly have less obligation to reduce their emissions. GDR allows for a clear and logical calculation of every country's climate obligation via a Responsibility Capacity Index. This index could then serve as a fair international basis for calculating climate costs or setting national caps on carbon emissions.*

* Paul Baer et al., *The Greenhouse Development Rights Framework: The Right to Development in a Climate Constrained World* (Berlin: Heinrich Böll Foundation, Christian Aid, EcoEquity and the Stockholm Environment Institute, 2008).

as well as different amounts of capacity to fix it. In general, it's the rich countries of the world who have the greatest responsibility for global warming, since they emit by far the most greenhouse gases per person. Since the beginning of the Industrial Revolution, the rich countries are responsible for roughly 70 percent of total emissions.[22] They also have the greatest capacity to fix it. This means that the bulk of carbon reductions must fall on the rich countries. In other words, the cap in those countries must be relatively lower than in poorer countries.

Imagine what would happen if quotas to emit carbon were distributed fairly to all the countries in the world. By "fair" I mean that these quotas would be based on a country's past emissions, as well as a measure of their financial ability. Rich countries would find themselves under pressure to reduce their emissions, so they would undoubtedly want to buy a large number of emissions quotas from poorer countries. If the Paris Agreement on climate change were restructured in this way, it would do more than save the environment. It would likely lead to a radical redistribution of wealth from rich countries to poor ones.

THE MARKET, THE STATE, AND FREEDOM

If there is one fundamental difference between neoliberal countries like the United States and social democratic countries like Sweden, it is a different understanding of the kind of institutions that promote our freedom. Is our freedom promoted by the state or the market?

The Statue of Liberty, "freedom fries," the New Hampshire licence plate motto *Live Free or Die*—these things reflect the central mythology of the United States. It is the *land of the free*. In this view, the United States is free because it is built upon a free market. The market gives people the freedom to work where they like, to buy what they desire, and to make whatever they want of their lives. Freedom makes the United States the land of opportunity. The market is essential to freedom, and the state—which interferes with private business and tells individuals how to run their lives— is its antithesis.

Newt Gingrich, a 2012 presidential nominee for the Republican Party, put it this way: "Freedom and the state are in perpetual conflict."[23] From this perspective, social democratic countries are bureaucratic "nanny" states, half-way down the road to totalitarianism.

But brush away the rhetoric, and it becomes clear that this view is pretty absurd. In the United States, 12 percent live in poverty, millions don't have health insurance, private universities cost $50,000 per year, mothers have no paid maternity leave, and so on.

In Sweden, 6 percent live in poverty, everyone has access to quality health care, university tuition is free, and parents receive sixteen months of well-paid parental leave. The United Nations consistently finds that the Nordic countries have the highest quality of life in the world. In 2013, Norway was number one in the world, while the United States was number sixteen.[24]

So we must ask ourselves, which society has more freedom? Are you free if you can't afford medical care? In his documentary about American healthcare, *Sicko*, Michael Moore interviews a man without health insurance who lost his middle and index finger in an accident. Since he did not have insurance the man had to choose which finger to re-attach—the index finger for $60,000, or his ring finger for $12,000. Is this freedom?

Are you free if you can't work because you are injured, disabled, or have mental health issues, and are forced to rely on welfare of roughly $500 per month? Are you free if you're a single mother with no daycare available? Are you free if you're a worker on a zero-hour contract?

Surely the essence of freedom is being able to live the life that you want. This requires meaningful security—so that you are free from poverty, hunger, homelessness, and destitution in your old age—and real opportunity. But the United States is worse on both of these accounts.

There is far less security in the United States than in Sweden for anyone who is not rich, because there are far fewer public services and universal protections. Furthermore, there is less opportunity in the form of social mobility in the United States than in Europe. The ladders of opportunity—such as education—are much less accessible. In the United States, men born into the bottom quintile (i.e., the poorest 20 percent of families) in 1958 had a 42 percent likelihood of ending up in the same position, which means the opportunity to move up is pretty low. Men born in northern Europe have a 25 to 30 percent likelihood. Only 8 percent of Americans manage the "rags to riches" climb from the bottom quintile to the top, whereas 11 to 14 percent do so in the social democracies.[25] On the basis of such facts Wilkinson concludes that "if Americans want to live the American dream, they should go to Denmark."[26]

The U.S. equation of a free market with free people is wrong. It ignores the crucial truth that freedom for the powerful means lack of freedom for everyone else. Freedom for the shark is death for the salmon.[27] The United States provides immense freedom in the market for rich people to pay little tax and for businesses to face little regulation. This creates freedom for a minority, but it shrinks freedom for everybody else. Sweden does the opposite. It is able to provide real freedom for everyone, because businesses and the wealthy are restrained by the state.

Whenever you hear talk about love of "freedom" and hatred of the "state" and "tyranny," you need to remember that it's not truly freedom that the speaker admires. If it was, they would support redistribution. Taking a dollar from a millionaire and giving it to a poor person is likely to increase the total freedom in society. This money will augment the freedom for the poor far more than it will decrease the freedom of the rich.

People who use this rhetoric aren't celebrating freedom itself, but the freedom of the rich. If they really hated tyranny, wouldn't they criticize the hugely authoritarian structure of modern corporations? It is redistribution of wealth that they oppose. But they can't publicly call for more money for the rich, so they espouse freedom and the free market instead.

We often witness conservatives criticizing legislation that will increase real freedom for the majority of the population, because it is not ideal for the rich. A striking example was in the 1930s, during the New Deal, when the U.S. Congress finally passed legislation providing social security (pensions, disability, and unemployment insurance) for all Americans. For the first time, every American could be assured they would not die of poverty in old age. How did Republicans respond? Congressman John Taber said the legislation would "enslave" society. Congressman Daniel Reed called it "the lash of the dictator." This has been a consistent theme throughout American history. In 2013, Republican senator Ron Johnson called President Obama's plan to provide health care insurance for all the "greatest assault on freedom in our lifetime."[28]

The conservative view of market freedom and state oppression is thus upside-down. A large number of regular, working-class people have been convinced that the employer is their friend, while the state bureaucrat is their enemy. The opposite is more accurate. The employer is the real enemy of working people, since their interests are structurally antagonistic. The state, at least when it works well, is the essential mechanism for protecting people. Shrinking the state undermines protection and restricts access to education, health care, pensions, daycare, maternity leave, and so on. Shrinking the state doesn't create more freedom, it creates less.

The ideal, of course, is to have a robust state but not an intrusive one telling us how to live our lives. For instance, there is no excuse for the British welfare state policy that prevented people living in social housing from painting their doors the colour of their choice.[29] I'm not advocating an authoritarian state, but a generous, caring one. Taxes need to be high enough to enable a welfare state to provide us with the infrastructure for good lives, to provide us with the basic freedoms of security and opportunity. This is real freedom. And it can only be provided by the state.

REBUILDING SOCIAL DEMOCRACY

Our most important short-term goal should be to rebuild social democracy. The market is useful for organizing the economy efficiently. But left to itself, it produces very unequal and oppressive outcomes. So it needs to be regulated by the state to provide security and equal opportunity for all—in a word, social justice.

The Nordic countries have been greatly successful in combining a market for economic growth with a strong state for social justice. From an economic perspective, social democracy is eminently viable. The GDP per capita of the Nordic states is just as high as the neoliberal ones ($29,600 compared to $29,500). Growth rates have been just as solid (2.05 percent of GDP per year compared to 2.3 percent over twenty years). And employment rates since the mid-2000s have been just as good if not better.[30]

From a justice perspective, social democracy is a vast improvement over neoliberalism. It provides more equality, less workplace domination, and greater opportunity and social mobility. It provides more security, better work-life balance, and better environmental outcomes (for instance, on windy days Denmark is able to generate 100 percent of its electricity from renewable sources—the highest level in the world).[31]

We know that social democracy can work. And we know that it is a far better alternative than the neoliberal norm. Let's build it now!

5

LONG-TERM ALTERNATIVES

TOWARD A DEMOCRATIC SOCIALISM

W HAT could it mean to actually move beyond capitalism? In the introduction we defined neoliberal capitalism as an economic system based on three fundamental features:

- a market system that is largely unregulated (or, more precisely, is regulated in ways that primarily benefit the wealthy) so that private profit is the overriding concern
- significant class inequality
- workplaces structured as undemocratic hierarchies

Last chapter we analyzed social democracy, which significantly improves on the unregulated market system. In this chapter, we look at two long-term goals—a guaranteed basic income and workplace democracy. These approaches would radically improve class inequality and workplace hierarchy, thereby transforming capitalism as we know it. These ideas for reform are not isolated proposals. They can be tied together to illustrate the contours of a full-blown alternative society: a society of democratic socialism.

Of course, changes of this magnitude are not likely to happen in the next year or two. But even if they are decades off, it is still worth talking about them now. It's important to have goals to strive for. If we don't know the direction we want to go, we're sure to end up somewhere we don't want to be.

WORKPLACE DEMOCRACY

We've seen that capitalist workplaces are fundamentally antagonistic and that unions are vital to protect workers against exploitation and domination. But when unions get powerful enough, workers can contradict the employer on more and more issues. Bosses start complaining that the workplace has become inflexible, with every decision becoming a new disagreement and source of conflict. And there is some truth to that.

The solution from the right has always been the same: get rid of the unions to restore the unilateral power of the boss. The social democratic left often proposes a stopgap reformist measure, demanding union rights to establish fair bargaining between the two parties. The real answer, though, is not to balance the power of the union and the boss, but to abolish the work antagonism itself. In other words, to get rid of the bosses' undemocratic power altogether.

In the words of the democratic socialist GDH Cole, writing in 1920:

> The employer complains, often with some justice, that he can no longer run his factory in his own way; but the Union on its side can only protect its members by hampering him, and has no positive power to run the factory in his stead.... The whole system is essentially one of unstable equilibrium, and it seems clear ... that there are only two possible alternatives. Either the power of the Union to impose restrictions must be broken; or it must be transformed from a negative into a positive power, and, instead of having only the brake

in their hands, the Trade Unions must assume control of the steering-wheel.[1]

What does it mean in practical terms to give workers the steering wheel? It means transforming hierarchical workplaces into democratic ones, that is, worker co-operatives. Worker co-ops are firms that are entirely governed by their own workers. One worker, one vote. There are no unelected managers or outside shareholders; no one in the firm has power over others simply because they were rich enough to buy shares.

Small co-ops can make their decisions in a participatory democratic fashion, sitting around the table. Larger co-ops, like any complex organization, require different departments, specialists, and managers to oversee and co-ordinate the whole. In a large organization it's impossible for everyone to directly participate in every decision so specialization and chains of command are necessary. But in a co-op, the crucial difference is that the top decision-makers are elected and accountable to the workers. It's a democracy, not a hierarchy.

Large co-ops thus resemble our political system, where we elect people to represent us. Workers elect representatives, whom they can also vote out. Just as we condemn states that lack democratic accountability—such as North Korea or Saudi Arabia—we should similarly condemn hierarchical workplaces. Just as we insist that people have a right to elect their political leaders, we should insist that workers have the right to elect their workplace leaders. The underlying rationale is the same. Power, if it is to be legitimate, must be made accountable to those affected by it.

One might object that workers don't have the necessary skills or expertise to be in charge of the workplace. But we don't think it's acceptable to disenfranchise citizens who aren't knowledgeable about politics. We don't, for example, make citizens take a politics test before they're allowed to vote. Similarly, there are no good grounds for disenfranchising workers in large firms simply because they don't know all the ins and outs of the entire firm.

Democracy doesn't require collective decision-making. It requires collective accountability. Experts and specialists are still required, but there's no reason that they can't be accountable. Robert Dahl is right when he says that experts should be kept "on tap, not on top."[2]

There are a few worker co-operatives in North America, but they are generally not well known. Consumer co-ops—such as John Lewis in the United Kingdom or MEC in Canada—are more common. But though they may be relatively progressive firms, they are not internally democratic; they are controlled not by the workers but by outside consumer-members. Worker co-ops—such as the Mondragon co-operatives in Spain[3]—are much more prominent in parts of Europe and South America. Northern Italy currently has the highest density of co-ops in the world. In the Emilia-Romagna region, worker co-ops constitute 13 percent of gross domestic product. They dominate in industries including construction, agriculture, food processing, wine making, transport, retail, and machine production.[4]

One worry might be that worker co-ops would be inefficient. People in North America, especially, have only experienced co-ops via the occasional small alternative coffee shop or radical do-it-yourself bike store. But over the last thirty years, economists have compiled substantial amounts of data comparing the performance of co-ops to conventional firms.[5] The evidence is clear: when they are scientifically compared, co-ops are found to be just as efficient as comparable capitalist firms. Co-ops have been found to have comparable levels of productivity everywhere that they have been studied—in Denmark, France, Italy, Spain, Sweden, United Kingdom, United States, and Uruguay.[6]

The efficiency of worker co-ops is not completely surprising. For one thing, workers are likely to have significantly more motivation to work hard than workers in conventional firms. As co-owners their motivation is enhanced by the fact that they receive a portion of the profits. In addition, co-ops are likely to have a better working environment. Workers are likely to feel more trust and less alienation. This has real payoffs: fewer sick days, less

The Mondragon Co-operatives, Spain

In the 1950s, in Mondragon in the Basque region of northern Spain, five workers under the guidance of a Catholic priest opened a small worker co-op. Several co-ops soon formed but found limited access to finance, since banks were generally hostile.

In 1959 a handful of local co-ops created their own co-operative bank—the Caja Laboral—and the co-ops began to thrive. By 2013 the Mondragon co-operative group included 103 co-ops, 74,000 people, and assets of a tremendous €34 billion.* The co-ops are leaders in a number of fields including industry, retail, and R&D. According to the *Economist*, the Irizar co-op is "probably now the most efficient coach builder in the world."† The efficiency of the co-ops is beyond dispute; most empirical studies find them to be more productive than similar conventional firms.‡

The Mondragon co-ops' principles include democratic organization, participation in management, solidarity, education, and social transformation. Each co-op is governed by its own internal workers, who elect the Governing Council and decide on their internal organization. Irizar, for example, has a flat organizational structure based on work teams, with no bosses but with "shared leadership."§ Each co-op sends delegates to the Co-operative Congress, which is like a mini-parliament.

Though Mondragon has struggled in recent years to deal with globalization without losing its core values, it is an inspiring example of the viability of large-scale workplace democracy.

* Mondragon Corporation, "Economic and Financial Highlights," www.mondragon-corporation.com (accessed May 2016).

† F.J. Forcadell, "Democracy, Cooperation and Business Success: The Case of Mondragon Corporacion Cooperativa," *Journal of Business Ethics* 56,3 (Feb. 2005), 256.

‡ For recent economic evidence, see Tom Malleson, "What Does Mondragon Teach Us About Workplace Democracy?," Advances in the Economic Analysis of Participatory and Labor-Managed Firms 14 (2013)

§ Greg MacLeod and Darryl Reed, "Mondragon's Response to the Challenges of Globalization: A Multi-Localization Strategy," in *Co-operatives in a Global Economy*, ed. Darryl Reed and J.J. McMurtry (Newcastle upon Tyne: Cambridge Scholars, 2009).

104

absenteeism, and less need to hire expensive managers to monitor every little thing.

One scholar recounts how in a plywood firm that was transformed from a co-op into a conventional firm in the Pacific Northwest, the first thing management did was quadruple the number of supervisors. "We need more foremen," explained the general manager, "because, in the old days, the shareholders [i.e., co-op members] supervised themselves.... They cared for the machinery, kept their areas picked-up, helped break up production bottlenecks all by themselves. That's not true anymore ... we've got to pretty much keep on them all of the time."[7]

Because co-ops have these advantages, some capitalist firms experiment with watered-down versions of workplace democracy—things like profit sharing or shared ownership. These are attempts to try to capture the efficiency benefits of co-operation without actually democratizing the firm.

Gregory Dow is a leader in the field of the economics of the firm. He concludes his comprehensive study of worker co-operatives with the following: "The general conclusion ... is that [co-ops] are not rare because they fail disproportionately often. Once created, they appear robust. Rather, they are rare because in absolute numbers they are created much less often than [capitalist firms]."[8]

So co-ops are completely viable from an economic perspective. From a social perspective, they are much superior. Worker co-ops are much more democratic. They also have much less wage inequality. They tend to compress the differences between workers' wages, so the highest paid usually make no more than three times the lowest paid. This is dramatically more egalitarian than capitalist firms. In social democratic countries, the average CEO makes 15 times the average wage. In the American context, the average CEO makes 200 times the average wage; indeed, in 2000 the gap was a stunning 531:1.[9] In this context, a CEO will make in a mere month's work the same amount as a worker will earn in thirty years—an entire career.

Co-ops also have far greater job security than conventional firms. They fire members only as a last resort. During recessions workers have the ability to collectively agree to reduce their hours or cut their wages in a fair manner. In a conventional firm, workers have no say, so managers will more likely sack a bunch of people outright.

None of this is to imply that co-ops are paradise. Work in a co-op is still work. And while co-op workers may have less stress from dealing with tyrannical managers, they may have more from the responsibility that comes from being a part owner. But co-ops are fundamentally better workplaces.

Why, then, haven't co-ops spread more? A common objection goes like this: Co-ops must be inefficient. If they were able to compete against regular firms, we'd see many more of them. Since the market is a level playing field, the scarcity of co-ops must mean that they can't survive the competition.

The market is not, however, a level playing field. Conventional firms have all kinds of advantages. Legally, it is far easier to set them up. Financially, conventional firms can get support from banks and stock markets. Educationally, huge amounts of societal resources go into schools and universities to train people to operate corporate businesses and give business advice, but almost no money goes into training people how to operate co-ops.

Given this lack of social support, it's no surprise that entrepreneurs are far more likely to set up conventional firms, which they are far more familiar with, than co-operatives. Yet there is nothing at all inevitable about this. If we as a society decided that we wanted more workplace democracy, we could easily put more resources into co-op banks, co-op schools, giving co-ops competitive tax breaks, and so on. These measures already exist in places like northern Italy and northern Spain, where co-ops flourish. If we want more workplace democracy, it is entirely possible to achieve it.

UNIVERSAL BASIC INCOME

The idea that every citizen should receive an unconditional or universal basic income (UBI) has a long history. It stretches back at least to Thomas Jefferson, the principal author of the U.S. Declaration of Independence. Yet it is only over the last twenty years or so that the idea has begun to emerge from the shadows. Particularly in Europe, it is becoming a more and more realistic proposal.[10] It is now official policy of Green Parties across Europe, and in 2016, 23 percent of the Swiss population voted in favour of introducing a basic income that would have given each adult about $20,000 per year. Although the referendum didn't pass, the result shows that the idea is becoming increasingly mainstream.

A UBI works as follows. The state guarantees every adult citizen a certain basic income each year. Everyone gets it, but most middle- and upper-class people pay it back (and more) in taxes. How is such a system different from welfare? It is unconditional. That means it is independent of your financial situation, and so is not "means-tested." There is no risk of receiving it one day and then losing it the next, depending on your employment situation. It is a guaranteed floor beneath which no citizen is allowed to fall.

Every society would have to limit its UBI based on how much it could afford. But ideally the amount would be sufficiently generous to constitute a living wage, perhaps in the range of $15,000 to $25,000 per year. High enough to support elderly or unemployed people at a non-luxurious but decent and dignified standard of living.

The fundamental purpose would be to create, for the first time, real economic security for all. In one fell swoop, extreme poverty would be abolished. Everyone would gain the security of knowing that no matter what transpires in their life, basic needs will be met. Such security would mean a massive expansion in real freedom. Workers would gain increased bargaining power as well as the ability to turn down crummy jobs because they would have an alternative. Female workers would no longer have to put up with a boss's sexual harassment. Mothers and elderly people would no longer have to face the stigma of lining up at the food bank to beg for meals. (The U.S. Department of Agriculture estimates that 48 million Americans rely on food stamps).[11] Unemployed people would no longer have to suffer the humiliation of explaining to welfare officers why they can't find a job. Students would be able to study the subjects that actually interest them without constantly worrying about the need to get a job at the end of it. Artists would be able to devote themselves to creativity and artistic innovation, instead of having to devote all their energy to waiting tables to get by.

Everyone would acquire significantly more freedom to shape their own lives. Instead of having to build their lives around the perennial search for money, people would be free to devote themselves to their passions, be they caregiving, activism, art, music, sport, spirituality, or rich social lives.

Think about what this means. A UBI is deeply anti-capitalist. The leash that ties each of us to the workplace would be severed. Work would no longer be the essential means to acquire the money to live. A UBI, at least at high levels, would constitute a revolution in what it means to be a human being. We would no longer be concerned above all else with the need to work for survival. A UBI thus marks a profound step in human evolution. It shifts the goalposts of life beyond the aim of living, to living well; beyond the goal of surviving, to flourishing.

On a practical level, a UBI is massively simpler than the existing hodgepodge of welfare programs, and so it could simplify the current welfare bureaucracy. It would also get rid of one of the biggest problems of the welfare system, the "poverty trap." Means-testing systems create a terrible poverty trap because as soon as you get a job, you immediately lose your welfare. Imagine you're getting $800 per month on welfare, and the only job available is a part-time minimum wage job offering $800 per month; there is no incentive to take the job. The welfare system is a trap because it creates disincentives for people to accept jobs. This would not happen with a UBI. Since it's unconditional, getting a job would not mean that you lose your UBI. So poor people would always make more money from getting a job.

Three common objections often come to mind.

- Won't a UBI make everyone want to stop work, making society as a whole far poorer?
- Isn't it unaffordable?
- Isn't it unfair to give money to lazy people—like surfers (for some reason surfers are the favourite example of philosophers in these discussions)—for doing nothing? Aren't they just parasites living off the wealth that hard-working people create?

The first objection is easy to meet. It seems very unlikely that a UBI of, say, $20,000, would cause most people to suddenly quit their jobs. Most people will still want to work, since they get some satisfaction from their job—a sense of purpose, an identity, the bonds of collegiality. And most people would want to earn significantly more money than the UBI provides.

It's true that people may work less, but from a free-time and environmental perspective, that's a good thing. It's also true that a UBI would make unpleasant jobs have to pay more. Workers wouldn't be desperate, so unpleasant jobs would have to pay better wages to entice workers. But that's a good thing too!

Experiments in Guaranteed Income

Between 1968 and 1980, the U.S. and Canadian governments conducted five experiments in guaranteed income (NJ; NC; Seattle, WA, and Denver, CO; Gary, IN; Winnipeg and Dauphin, MB). Groups were given income guarantees between 50 to 150 percent of the poverty line, and compared with control groups who were not.

The guaranteed income was associated with significant improvements in education (better attendance, teacher ratings, and test scores), particularly among poor families in the rural south. In addition, the guaranteed income was associated with a reduction in dangerous births of low-weight babies.

Economically, the fears that a guaranteed income would be a disaster proved unfounded. There was no evidence that people receiving the income simply quit their jobs. Nor did a reduction in work effort make the cost of the program unaffordable. However, the experiments did find that, unsurprisingly, giving people money created a disincentive to work: they predicted that if an income guarantee became government policy, primary income earners would likely reduce their workload by up to 7 percent.

This fact, hardly surprising, was enough to kill the programs politically (on conservative grounds that anything that discourages work must be bad). But in many cases reduced work is actually a good thing and shows that the program is working well, since a central point of the UBI is to free workers from the necessity of undesirable or exploitative work. For example, the experiments found that the largest change in work hours came from female workers—who made a slower re-entry into the labour market after absences (such as pregnancy).*

* Robert Levine et al., "A Retrospective on the Negative Income Tax Experiments: Looking Back at the Most Innovate Field Studies in Social Policy," in *The Ethics and Economics of the Basic Income Guarantee*, ed. Karl Widerquist, Michael Anthony Lewis, and Steven Pressman (Hampshire: Ashgate, 2005); Karl Widerquist, "A Failure to Communicate: What (If Anything) Can We Learn from the Negative Income Tax Experiments?," *The Journal of Socio-Economics* 34,1 (Feb. 2005).

Is a UBI affordable? At a very low level, say, $100 per year, of course it's affordable, but it's also not much use. At the other extreme, a UBI of $100,000 per year would require more taxes than a country's entire GDP. That's completely unaffordable. For a UBI to have liberatory effects, it needs to be above the poverty level. This would require a UBI in the range of $15,000 to $25,000. Instituting a UBI at that level might well require increasing taxes by 10 percent or so.[12] This is undeniably expensive, but not impossible. It would depend on whether the majority of the population could be persuaded to go along with it.

The major issue here is not whether a UBI is theoretically affordable, but whether it's the best use of our money. Economic security is a fundamentally important goal, but a UBI is not the only way to provide it. Remember that giving cash is only one method of providing people with security. We could also guarantee everyone a job (for example, by having the government be an employer of last resort). We could also provide high-quality public services to those who need them (for example, free university education for students, free daycare for parents, high levels of support for people with disabilities, affordable housing for people living in poverty, and so on). So while a UBI has a lot to recommend it, we should be cautious here. Ultimately, we can't decide the best way forward without carefully comparing the costs and benefits of a UBI with other possibilities.

The third objection is harder to address, and I should admit up front that I do not know what the right answer is. On the one hand, the accusation that non-workers are parasites is inaccurate. You often hear rich people saying, *I worked hard for my money. The bum on welfare is just lazy. Why should I support them?* But as we've seen, the vast majority of the income that anyone makes is not due to personal effort, but to their good fortune to live in a productive economic system that has been constructed by the collective efforts of generations before us. Here is Herbert Simon, one of the most influential social scientists of the twentieth century, addressing a North American audience:

Let me pose a simple question. Consider the income that you or your family now earn . . . and compare it with the income that you would expect to earn if you were equally hardworking members of Chinese or Indian society, or the society of any other Third World nation. I expect that for most of you, the difference between the two incomes is one or more orders of magnitude, at least 10 to 1 and perhaps even more than 100 to 1.

Now, I would like you to consider the causes for the gap between the 10 and the 1 or the 100 and the 1. How much of it do you wish to attribute to your superior energy, motivation, and application of effort as compared with your Third World counterparts? And how much do you wish to attribute to your good luck or good judgment in being born in, or joining, the highly productive and democratic American society?

If we are very generous with ourselves, I suppose we might claim that we "earned" as much as one fifth of it. The rest is the patrimony associated with being a member of an enormously productive social system, which has accumulated a vast store of physical capital, and an even larger store of intellectual capital—including knowledge, skills, and organizational know-how held by all of us—so that interaction with our equally talented fellow citizens rubs off on us both much of this knowledge and this generous allotment of unearned income.[13]

This means that the claim that we can divide society into "hard workers" and "parasites" is nonsense. We are *all* dependent on a massive social inheritance. True, some may work harder than others. But in the scheme of things, individual income in rich countries is mostly a result of tremendous historical luck. Once we see this, it becomes clear that a UBI isn't about creating parasites. It's about redistributing the immense luck of living in a rich social system to those who are somewhat less lucky.

On the other hand, the UBI does strike many people, even on the left, as deeply unfair. The notion of paying people who are not contributing at all goes against the grain of the cherished idea of reciprocity. Everyone should "chip in"; we're all in this together.

One response is to say that we need to get over this need for reciprocity. Perhaps we could try to adopt an ethic of unconditional generosity. Another approach is to insist that a UBI should be conditional on chipping in in some way. That might mean traditional work, but it could also include contributing to society through volunteering, political activism, caregiving, or art. Such a system would jibe with a sense of reciprocity. If they knew that others were contributing too, people working in traditional jobs would be less likely to feel taken advantage of.

A conditional UBI would exclude people from receiving it and so be cheaper. On the other hand, it would be more difficult to operate since it requires continued monitoring of people. An unconditional UBI requires no bureaucracy because you don't have to spend time and resources looking for people cheating the system. It's also far less degrading. It doesn't require intrusive interviews from welfare officers investigating, for example, whether the caregiving you are doing for your grandparent is really necessary. It doesn't require begging and scraping to get the money. A cheque just arrives every month in the mail.

This is a complicated issue because at root there's a tension between two ethical ideas: unconditional support of fellow citizens, versus reciprocity and obligation toward fellow citizens. There's also the pragmatic issue of what kind of UBI is most likely to gain societal support and get political parties behind it. Is it worth watering down an ideal if doing so makes it more likely to get a policy through parliament?

My own stance is that a conditional basic income seems far more likely to win widespread approval, so that's what we should aim for. The threshold for what counts as contributing should be kept low enough that the people who really need the support— single mothers, elderly people, and so on—don't have to jump through too many hoops to get it. A good strategy in the short term is to fight to get some kind of basic income on the books, even if it's conditional and even if it starts by offering only small amounts of money. From there it will likely be much easier to deepen and expand it.

DEMOCRATIC SOCIALISM

To put it all together, consider this stunning thought experiment. Imagine if tomorrow the U.S. population decides to rearrange its economy to fairly share out work, income, and leisure. It raises taxes, redistributes income, and spreads out working hours evenly across the population. It would be possible to provide public services as generous as Sweden's in addition to a UBI, while still providing every worker with the same median income that exists today. Moreover, each worker would need to work only three hours per day![14]

Of course, the economy is more complex than this, and getting to this point would involve a huge political fight. But the numbers add up. Our economies are productive enough that the material basis for a fundamentally different kind of society already exists. The constraints to creating a good life for all are no longer what's physically possible. The constraints are those of politics. It's no longer a question of producing enough for survival; it's a question of distributing the produce in a fair and decent way. The issue today is a struggle over what powerful people desire versus what regular people are organized enough to demand.

In the remainder of this chapter, I will illustrate one model of what a democratic socialist society could actually look like. But before doing so, let me address a couple of likely objections.

The first is whether it's useful to bother with long-term visions of society. Isn't this utopian? Well, yes and no. The word "utopia" has a positive and a negative meaning. The negative side is that of unrealistic fantasy. To say that something is utopian in this sense is to say that it is simply impossible. But utopia also has a positive side—a hope and optimism that things can be fundamentally different than they are now. So I agree that we should avoid dreaming about the impossible. But I disagree that we should abandon the positive sense of utopia, the hope and optimism that there are alternatives.

The goal, in other words, is to try to envision what sociologist Erik Olin Wright calls "real utopias." [15] These are structures and institutions of society that are realistic, based on empirical evidence, and conscious of the constraints and tradeoffs that always limit human designs. At the same time, the institutions are designed to embody, as much as possible, freedom, equality, and solidarity.

Models of real utopias are not meant to be blueprints that describe exactly what a future society will look like. Society is far too complex for that. But they can usefully serve as a compass, orienting our goals and providing an overall direction for our activism.

The second objection is whether it's worth talking about socialism at all. There is, after all, an ugly history associated with the word, and few words today are as polluted. The right has done a remarkable job of making the word evoke images of the gulags, military marches, show trials, food lines—grey, drab, tyrannical, and totalitarian.

It is true that brutal tyrants and dictators have done terrible things in the name of socialism. We've seen Joseph Stalin in Soviet

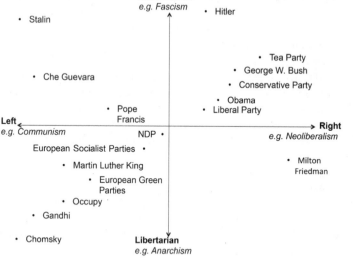

LONG-TERM ALTERNATIVES

Figure 5.1. Political Compass

The basic design for this political compass comes from http://politicalcompass.org. This particular version is the author's.

Russia, Mao Tse-tung in revolutionary China, Pol Pot in Cambodia, Kim Jong Il in North Korea, all claiming allegiance to socialism while suppressing democracy and squelching dissent. But the democratic socialism that I'm talking about is as far from the authoritarian socialism of these leaders as it is from the "national socialism" of Hitler's Nazis.

This can be a confusing point to understand. It's natural to think that if both political positions are "socialist"—if they're both "on the left"—they must have a lot in common. But politics is not simply a matter of left versus right. It's also a matter of democratic (or libertarian) versus authoritarian. The left–right axis focuses on whether the economy should be controlled by the community or the state in some way, as leftists want, or by private individuals, as the right desires. A second vital aspect of politics is how authoritarian it should be. Should people follow orders and respect authority, or be critical of authority and insist on individual freedom and democratic self-management? An accurate political spectrum, in other words, is not one-dimensional, but two-dimensional.

To give an example, Hitler is often thought of as the extreme right. But his economic policies were actually quite centrist. His policies were extreme not in economics but in authoritarianism. In his willingness to mass slaughter his political enemies, he has more in common with people like Stalin than a simple left–right delineation would indicate.

Referring to Figure 5.1, the version of socialism that I am talking about occupies the bottom left of this political compass. Soviet-style socialism is found on the top left. So we can see that these positions have little in common. They are about as far apart from each other as the United Kingdom or Canada today (centre) are from the Nazis (top right).

The core of democratic socialism is the values of empathy, solidarity, generosity, and kindness—and the desire to replace social relations of hierarchy and violence with relations of mutuality. When we think of democratic socialism, we shouldn't think of such figures as Stalin or Mao. Rather, we should think of Helen Keller and Albert Einstein, George Orwell and Bertrand Russell, Mahatma Gandhi and Nelson Mandela.

A Real Alternative

So what would a democratic socialist society actually look like?

In the political sphere, the first-step reforms are obvious enough: tighter restrictions on the amount of money that can be contributed to political parties, and limiting the revolving door between government and big business. In addition, we need proportional representation to replace the current winner-take-all system, so that every vote is actually counted. More ambitiously, the most important idea for fundamentally improving the political system is *decentralization*. The more that decision-making power is decentralized to cities and neighbourhood councils, the more people can directly participate in decisions that affect their lives. We should strive to implement participatory democracy wherever the scale of the issue concerned makes it feasible to do so. Local-level participatory democracy should be nested within higher levels of representative democracy. Good examples of participatory democracy include Participatory Budgeting in Brazil (where neighbourhoods decide on the kind of public spending they want), and the Communal Councils in Venezuela.[16] In settler countries like Canada and Australia, this decentralization must go hand-in-hand with the creation of enhanced political sovereignty for indigenous peoples over a variety of issues. This should include things like increased autonomy over politics and local education, as well as co-management of lands and resources.

In the economic sphere, we can imagine an economy built on the following characteristics.[17]

- There is a *market that is highly regulated by the state.* The state provides excellent public services, such as life-long free education and retraining, and universal health care. It engages in redistributive taxation to fund the public services and to reduce inequality. The state regulates the market, ensuring that businesses respect health and safety protocols, provide parental leave, and so on. It also engages in public investment in areas that businesses typically avoid, such as infrastructure and other public goods. And it protects the environment by establishing caps on natural resource use, conservation areas, and so on.
- Progressive taxation funds a generous *unconditional basic income.*
- Most firms are structured as *worker co-operatives.* The workers elect their own management and decide on the patterns of remuneration. Workers enjoy government-mandated rights to flexible work and a cultural

norm of part-time work (perhaps in the range of fifteen to twenty hours per week). Firms get loans from
public community banks. These banks are funded by the
city they are in and mandated to support the co-ops that
have the most potential to grow economically, as well
as the most potential to provide for social needs. They
might, for example, promote green businesses.

How would such a system function? People would apply for
jobs in the normal way. Co-ops would try to make money in the
market, just as firms do today. They would be free to pay their
workers equal wages or not. (Experience with co-ops indicates
that differentials will not usually exceed 3:1.) Co-ops looking to
expand would apply for loans from their local public bank. Those
that are innovative and successful at responding to the population's demands would grow and prosper. Successful firms would
make more money than their competitors, thus providing incentives to work hard.

High levels of taxation, however, would prevent the rich from
becoming super-rich, and would also pay for excellent public services. Firms that produce things that no one wants would go out
of business. Their workers would need to find new jobs, but they
would do so in a context of strong public services and a UBI to fall
back on.

There would still be competition, which is useful for keeping firms accountable to what the population wants. But no one
wins majestically or loses tragically. No one becomes rich enough
to acquire power over others, or poor enough to go hungry or
lose their health care. The market competition here resembles a
friendly sports race more than a life-or-death battle.

What can we say about this kind of society? The first thing to
notice is that there is nothing at all totalitarian about this kind of
socialism. On the contrary, it's a radically democratic society. It's far
more democratic, in fact, than contemporary neoliberal capitalism.
Democracy exists not only in the state but also in the workplaces

and financial institutions. The state doesn't tell anyone where to work. In fact, individuals have much greater freedom than today. They apply for the jobs they want, leave when they wish to, and choose how many hours they want to work to suit their life plans. The state doesn't direct businesses in how they must operate. The co-ops are self-managing and take orders from no one, beyond standard taxation and regulation (ensuring health and safety, parental leave rights, flextime rights, non-discriminatory practices, and so on).

And while this society is hugely different from our own, it is not at all a utopian fantasy. There is nothing unrecognizable or totally foreign to our understanding of how the world works. On the contrary, we are already familiar with each of its core characteristics.

We have extensive familiarity with regulated markets, for example, in Nordic social democracy. A handful of small guaranteed income experiments have shown encouraging results. We have substantial case studies of worker co-operatives. Democratic banks are the least well known feature. But even here we have experience with close siblings, such as state-owned public banks, credit unions, and Mondragon's Caja Laboral. So real-world experience gives us good reasons to think that such an economy would indeed be workable.

I'm not claiming that this kind of economic system would be perfect. It would not on its own deal with non-economic problems such as patriarchy, ableism, and racism. There would still be a degree of material inequality, but there would be no class inequality, since inheritance taxes would prevent privilege from being passed on from parent to child. Everyone would have equal opportunity to go to excellent public schools and universities. With free education and training, adult workers would be free to retrain at any point to try to increase their salaries.

Allowing some minimal inequality in wages provides incentives for people to work hard. But the kind of inequality that exists in this society is fundamentally different than in ours. There are some differences in income, but not in power or social status. In those respects, everyone is equal. One person may choose to work longer hours to buy a fancier car than another. But the institutions in society have been fundamentally democratized. No matter how much people work, their money can never be translated into unaccountable power over other people.

This democratic socialist society would still have traces of unfairness. For example, a co-op may become rich or broke through the sheer luck of changing consumer preferences. But this is a minor problem in such a society. High levels of taxation and the UBI would redistribute the effects of luck by providing security against misfortune. People in this society have agreed to share one another's fate.[18] The minor issues of unfairness that inevitably come from having a market system are, it seems to me, far outweighed by the practical usefulness of using a market system to organize allocation in a way that is efficient and democratically responsive to the population.

A society doesn't need to be perfect to make it worth fighting for. The democratic socialist society I've described would be immeasurably better than our current one. The values of freedom, equality, and solidarity would no longer be mere words. They would reflect the institutional reality of the economy.

There would be equal freedom in work. There would be equal freedom from work. People would have guaranteed security from want and deprivation, and real opportunity to develop their own lives in whichever direction they so desire. There would also be environmental sustainability. The economy could function safely within the surrounding ecosystem, without trampling over it.

This may not be a society of perfection, but it would be one of profound progress.

6

SOMETHING TO FIGHT FOR

THERE ARE
MANY ALTERNATIVES

TAKE A SECOND to picture what your life would have been like if you were living a few generations back, say in the 1930s. Imagine living as a poor person at that time in Canada, the United States, or Europe.[1] Working ten-hour days in some dark, dank factory, side by side with teenagers and elderly people, doing dangerous work with no protective equipment. Feeling constantly worried that if you lose your job, or get sick, you'll have nowhere to turn but the soup kitchens.

Recall what it must have been like when wealthy people ran their businesses like petty kingdoms, strutting down the hallway shouting commands, with the power to fire anyone at any moment for any reason. Workers were left in a perpetual state of fear. The same deadening work, day after day, with little hope for things to get better. Few holidays or possibilities for education. Feeling continually desperate to save enough money to support your family in old age, since there is no help to fall back on.

Now imagine a socialist activist at this time talking to their neighbours and co-workers. They point out the problems, discuss alternatives, and incite people to come to meetings to organize to do something about them. The response would be entirely predictable. *Stop dreaming! This is how things have always been. It's natural to arrange society in this way. If you try to change things you'll only end up making them worse—look at Russia!*

The status quo would be pervasive and overwhelming. Newspapers would regurgitate conventional warnings that conservatives declare to be the wisdom of experience. The regular person on the street would think these cautions are common sense. Wealthy academics and experts would write books on them. *There is no alternative. The system works well. Any attempt to change it would be disastrous.*

In such a situation, a good-hearted person who wants things to change may feel like an ant against an implacable boulder of public opinion. It seems just too big to move.

But flash forward forty or so years, and conditions, particularly in countries like Sweden, are barely recognizable. Society has been fundamentally transformed. The rebels and radicals didn't accept TINA and retreat into the confines of their private lives. Instead they sought out like-minded people and formed activist organizations. They helped build unions at work, and the unions eventually grew into social movements, which in time blossomed into political parties. Bit by bit, through blood and tears and tireless commitment, the foundations of society were reshaped. Guaranteed health care for all, free university, pension security, co-determination at work, parental leave, health and safety regulations, unfair dismissal protections, and on and on. All resulting in unprecedented social mobility and quality of life.

Think, too, about the struggles for gender or racial justice. When the suffragettes were fighting for recognition in the early 1900s, they gathered in tiny groups in private living rooms. They were enormously unpopular, trying to overturn a norm of female inferiority that for thousands of years had been ingrained as true and natural. Their protests led to imprisonment. Their hunger strikes were met with forced feedings. And yet, little by little, their movements grew until women won the vote.

In 1958, Ella Baker moved to Atlanta to become the first and only full-time staff member for the Southern Christian Leadership Congress, led by Martin Luther King. There was no office, no phone, no staff. White supremacy was institutionalized in schools, workplaces, and neighbourhoods. Black activists were regularly harassed, jailed, and beaten. Mainstream politicians, like the governor of Alabama, could proudly declare their commitment to "segregation now, segregation tomorrow, segregation forever." Despite all this, U.S. civil rights activists mobilized tirelessly. They eventually won the Civil Rights and Voting Registration Acts of 1964 and 1965.

Even when the status quo feels unmovable, the efforts of committed activists can radically change society. As American anthropologist Margaret Mead famously put it, "Never doubt that a small group of thoughtful, committed, citizens can change the world. Indeed, it is the only thing that ever has."

IDEAS FOR A TRANSITION

There are no real secrets about the core ingredients of political transition. Every influential movement requires two building blocks: powerful ideas of alternatives, and activist energy to build campaigns and foster social movements.

First, activists have to develop ideas of alternatives so that we can combat the ideology of TINA. Whenever elites and conservatives say *there is no alternative*, we must be prepared to respond with *there are many alternatives!*

When they say that there is no alternative to inequality, we point to the Nordic countries and propose progressive taxation, inheritance tax, enhanced public spending on welfare, expansion of trade unions, solidaristic bargaining, active labour market policy, accessible education, and worker participation in management. When they say that there is no alternative to workplace hierarchy, we propose stronger unions, better regulation, co-determination, and in particular we point to worker co-ops, like Mondragon. When they say there is no alternative to consumerism, we point to the history of practically every culture prior to capitalism. We propose norms of part-time work and restrictions on advertising in public spaces, and insist on the superior happiness and freedom that is offered by a life of reduced work and abundant leisure.

When they say there is no alternative to corporate globalization, we insist on the alternatives of corporate oversight, global labour standards, consumer boycotts, and protectionist tariffs. And when they say there is no alternative to environmental destruction, we point to indigenous peoples living sustainably throughout the ages. We propose alternatives of cap-and-trade, environmental taxes, conservation areas, and a strengthened Paris Agreement on climate change.

So the first building block for political change is to articulate clear proposals for alternatives that can inspire. As the French novelist Victor Hugo once said, "there is no greater power on earth than an idea whose time has come."[2] Alternative visions will only gain mass appeal if they seem both attractive and feasible. Activists need to present coherent visions of short- and long-term reforms that are logically connected to each other. It needs to be demonstrated how immediate feasible changes could naturally lead to more profound changes down the road.

This was something that we in the Occupy movement did badly. The Occupy protests spread like wildfire in 2011 and 2012. From a small protest on Wall Street the movement quickly spread to 951 cities in 82 countries around the world.[3] But a common and mostly fair criticism was that the protesters did not present a clear understanding of the movement's aims and goals. There was a confusing mishmash of disparate ideas, such as more public spending on health care side by side with calls for global revolution now.

Imagine if the protests had coalesced around a few simple, realistic demands. For example, around an immediate small financial transaction tax (also known as the "Robin Hood tax"), and increased progressive taxation on the 1 percent. Activists could then have painted a picture of how a financial transaction tax is a necessary first step toward regulating the banks on the road to democratizing the economy, or started a discussion about how raising taxes on the rich is a step toward creating a stronger welfare system, on the way to an even bigger goal of an unconditional basic income.

If we had started with demands such as these, we might have won immediate gains. Such victories would likely have brought more energy into the movement, as sceptics came to see the tangible results that activism can deliver. Instead, Occupy's demands remained hazy and vague. The energy and excitement of the protests gradually dissipated.

It's particularly important to come up with powerful long-term ideas for what are sometimes called revolutionary reforms. These are reforms that could slowly but fundamentally change the way society works. Such ideas are crucial for galvanizing people to work toward shared goals. Among the many possibilities, in the previous chapter we focused on two: workplace democracy and UBI. One further idea that has profound possibilities for radically altering society is the Meidner Plan. This plan suggests a way to organize a slow but radical transformation of society.

Rudolf Meidner was the chief economist of the largest Swedish union in the 1970s. He proposed that all firms with more than fifty workers should be obligated to create new shares worth 20 percent of annual company profits, which would be set aside as "wage-earner funds."[4] These funds would be controlled by each firm's workers until their value reached a size of 20 percent of the firm's total value. At this point, control would shift outside of the firm and the funds would be governed by regional public bodies controlled by the trade unions.

The underlying idea is that year after year a portion of the firm's profits are passed into wage-earner funds, which could then be used for socially responsible investment in the public interest. Every year more company shares would be controlled by the wage-earner funds. It was estimated that firms making 10 percent profit per year would become majority worker-controlled within thirty-five years. Thus the investment process would slowly and cumulatively pass into the hands of workers and their representatives.

The plan came very close to being implemented. It even received support from the ruling Social Democratic Party for a time. Ultimately, though, it lost the battle of public opinion and was significantly watered down. Business opposed it, unsurprisingly, but public scepticism centred on handing over so much economic control to trade unions. Had the funds been set up more transparently and democratically—for example, if they were controlled by community representatives rather than the unions themselves—it is likely that the plan would have passed. And Sweden would have become the world's first economic democracy.[5]

Although the Meidner Plan was developed for a specific Swedish context, the core idea remains very powerful. It's easy to imagine a variant that we might call an Incremental Democratization Plan.[6] It would have two distinct streams. In the banking stream, a portion of profits from private banks would be cumulatively placed under the control of newly established public community banks. In the business stream, a portion of profits from private firms would be cumulatively placed under the control of an internal workers' trust, governed on a one-worker, one-vote basis. This trust could then serve as a basis for workers to buy out their firms in order to transform them into worker co-operatives, if the workers so desired.

It is the cumulative nature of the plan that makes it such a powerful vehicle for societal transition. Over time, such a plan would gradually and non-violently transform the economy. It would replace private banks with public ones and private firms with worker-owned co-ops. This would at one stroke democratize finance and democratize workplaces—two fundamental goals of economic democracy. Although such changes would be gradual, the cumulative effect would be massive. Indeed, they would be revolutionary.

ORGANIZE

Ideas provide the inspiration and direction for political transition. But unless they are channelled into concrete social organizing they remain ephemeral. Unless they are used to animate concrete kinds of activism, they have no impact.

Few people, however, feel motivated enough to engage in activism. Most of us feel powerless and all of us feel busy. We live in societies whose political processes are perverted by money and corporate lobbyists. Corporate power is massive, and conservative ideology is dominant. It can be hard to believe that we as individuals are able to effect any meaningful change. But we all possess some influence in the different spheres of our lives. The key is to recognize the areas in which we can exert this influence and push forward, bit by bit, in each of them.

As consumers we can influence corporate practices by refusing to buy products produced in sweatshops and by insisting on environmental and union-made products. You can visit sites such as Fairtrade International (www.fairtrade.net) to find a country-specific Fairtrade organization in your area. For example, Ethical Consumer (www.ethicalconsumer.org), a U.K. organization, offers tips on using consumer pressure to make global business more sustainable. And Better World Shopper reports on companies' human rights, environmental, animal protection, community, and social justice records (www.betterworldshopper.org).

As workers the most vital thing we can do is join a union. From there, we can use our collective power to push management to extend worker rights and freedoms.

As citizens we can vote for progressive candidates. In first-past-the-post systems like Canada and the United States, it usually makes sense to vote for the most progressive candidate who actually has a chance of winning. This may involve holding our noses if they aren't our ideal candidate. Although if political parties receive public funds based on their percentage of votes, there can be an argument that voting for more radical parties may enable them to compete later. In first-past-the-post systems, a vote for anyone other than the winner is simply a wasted vote. In proportional electoral systems, on the other hand—like in Austria, Denmark, the Netherlands, Norway, Spain, Sweden, and many other places—every vote counts. Every party gets exactly the same proportion of members of parliament as the number of votes they received. So if a radical left or green party gets 10 percent of the votes, they will get 10 percent of the seats. (They would likely get nothing in a first-past-the-post system, because their votes would be spread out across different areas and so would not win any particular riding).

Moreover, our potential to influence society as citizens extends far beyond voting. Voting takes a couple of minutes every couple of years. We should do it. It's important to use every morsel of influence that we have. But far more important is getting involved in real activism. American novelist Alice Walker is right when she says, "Activism is my rent for living on the planet."

Political activism can take many shapes—joining a consumer boycott, organizing a union drive, working for a non-governmental organization, volunteering with a charity, becoming a member of a political party, or joining an activist group. Of course, we are all busy with the minutiae of our lives. But activists throughout history—from the anti-apartheid struggles in South Africa to the civil rights struggle in the United States—had much harder lives than most people in the rich countries today. They faced more severe material pressure and risked greater repression, and yet still found time to organize. Not everyone needs to be engaged in politics full-time. But all of us can at least be part-timers, putting a little bit of activist energy into each sphere of our lives. All of us can ask ourselves: How am I contributing to the struggle as a consumer, as a worker or caregiver, as a citizen?

While engagement in each sphere is important, I want to emphasize the special urgency of grassroots activism. It could be volunteering at a soup kitchen or joining a militant anti-poverty organization. Such activism is the foundation, the very bricks and mortar, of every social movement. If we are to challenge neoliberal capitalism, far more people need to devote some of their time to this kind of organizing.

What kind of grassroots activism is best? Is it better to join an activist group (like Greenpeace or the Ontario Coalition Against Poverty) or a political party like the Greens in the United Kingdom? Is it better to work outside the system or within it? These are old and complicated questions, and I think it's probably best to resist simple answers.

An old-school puritanism would insist that there is only one kind of real or important activism. Too often segments of the left have declared that real activism must focus exclusively on winning state power. But while this approach has its advantages, it also has its problems. As the Russian anarchist Peter Kropotkin once said, "You mean to conquer the state, but the state will end up conquering you."[7] This was his way of warning that power corrupts.

Again and again, strong social movements get caught up in the game of political power—trying to win this seat or appease that politician. As a result, their vitality gets drained and their goals become compromised. In the United States, for example, nothing has been more successful at dissipating the energy and vitality of social movements than absorbing them into the Democratic Party.[8]

Other segments of the left have insisted that we should not focus on the state at all. Rather, we should focus on building autonomous alternatives as part of civil society. It's possible, say proponents of this point of view, to change the world without taking power.[9] But the problem is, without the power of the state, it's very hard to restrain the power of the capitalists. And without the resources of the state, it's very difficult to provide for needy people or foster the growth of alternative institutions.

Social movements, like any living thing, need care and support to grow. Movements require legal support in changing laws. They require financial support in paying for new services. And they require cultural support in spreading new ideas. The state is usually the only source capable of providing such support.

If activists are the farmers of social movements, so to speak, the state is indispensable in providing the fertilizer and irrigation.

So I suggest that we be tolerant and pluralistic about the kind of activism that people do. We need autonomous grassroots activists building alternative structures and new kinds of institutions. But we also need people working in political parties and inside the system so that the state will not be overtly hostile to social movements but willing to facilitate the growth of new institutions. The key is for the state to facilitate but not command; not to make decisions for others but to provide people with the tools to make their own decisions.[10]

What is the best way for activists to organize? Looking around progressive organizations today, we can see two standard models. Some NGOs and charities model themselves on the governance structures of corporations. They organize hierarchically, with a board of governors at the top and a strict top-down chain of command. This is done partly out of a desire to appear "legitimate" or "serious" to the powers that be. It also shows a lack of imagination regarding alternatives. It's distressing how many NGOs aren't even aware of the worker co-op model.

Accepting the corporate form as the only way to structure an organization is to surrender to the ideology of TINA. It is to succumb to the idea that having unaccountable bosses on the one side and disempowered workers on the other is somehow natural or inevitable.

For much of the twentieth century, the dominant model of the activist group was the authoritarian socialist one. This model was based on the Russian revolutionary Vladimir Ilyich Lenin's idea of the "vanguard," a small group of professional activists organized like a mini-army.[11] The party leaders at the top do the thinking and planning, while the activist foot soldiers at the bottom follow the orders with iron discipline. The vanguard is meant to lead the people in the right direction. It assumes that the people, left to their own devices, are unable to realize what is in their true interests.[12]

Lenin developed this secret military structure in a Tsarist context when political organizing was illegal. But in the context of Western democratic countries, this strikes me as a terrible model. The fundamental problem is that no activist structure based on an army is ever likely to magically wither away to leave a democratic society.[13] Indeed, Lenin's vanguard—and his top-down political structures more generally—grew naturally into the dictatorship that followed under Stalin. Even if the vanguard wins, you'll be left with a society resembling an army. On this issue, anarchist Mikhail Bakunin was right when he criticized the authoritarian socialists: "If you pull a sapling out of the ground, cut off all the leaves and branches, and make it into a club, you cannot expect to plant it back in the ground and have it grow into a beautiful tree."

Instead, we need organizations to embody, in their structures and cultures, the ends we hope to reach through them. If we want a world that is radically democratic—egalitarian, empowering, participatory, based on mutual aid and solidarity—then we must organize in ways that reflect these politics. The slogan widely attributed to Gandhi—that we must be the change we want to see in the world—is right. Our activist organizations must be micro-cosms of the world that we wish to live in.

Organizing in a radically democratic way does not only mean internally democratic, though that is vital. It must also be externally democratic in the sense of being deeply rooted in the broader community. If activist organizations are to grow and flourish, they need to be open and accessible to new people. Leftist groups too often shut themselves off from the outside world. They become inward looking, insular, and preoccupied with their own moral righteousness. They find themselves talking in a vocabulary filled with jargon and angry rhetoric. They discuss abstract issues far removed from the concrete concerns of their neighbours. They look down at anyone who disagrees with their analysis for not being "radical enough"—and then, remarkably, express surprise when no new people show up to their events.

Activists should always remember that thousands and thousands of people pass through radical groups at some point in their lives. Our movements remain small for the simple reason that people don't stay. The main reason people drop out of activism is not campaign failures but interpersonal conflicts. People drop out not because they lose faith in social justice, but because they become disillusioned with activist spaces, which too often lose the sense of joy, freedom, and belonging that so many of us want. Instead of being places of creativity and human connection, they disintegrate into sites of work, stress, and interpersonal antagonism. Instead of feeling like a holistic part of the community woven into the fabric of people's lives, the intense urgency to respond to the latest crisis, combined with insularity and detachment from the mainstream, can lead to activist spaces becoming inflexible and inaccessible, unwelcoming to the disabled, the foreign-speaking, children, and elders. If activist organizations are to grow and flourish they need to be open and accessible to new people. They need to offer people real experiences of the sort of peaceful, kind, egalitarian relationships that are often lacking in the broader hierarchical society.

This can only be done by building community spaces that, although serious, are also fun, joyful, and free. Our activist spaces need to be places that we actually want to live. They need to be full of exciting ideas, new ways of interacting, respectful disagreement, empathy, compassion, mutual aid, even love. It is not for nothing that the early civil rights activists in the United States—some of the most talented activists the world has ever seen—used to say that you can tell the strength of a movement by how loud it was singing.

RISE UP!

We live in an era of profound apathy. The apathy is generated, on the one side, by the distractions of glittery consumerism, and on the other, by precarious insecurity that fosters inward selfishness and outward cynicism. It is an apathy cemented by the never-ending whispers that *there is no alternative*.

But TINA is a lie and always has been. If our ancestors had believed it, we would not be where we are today. The rights and freedoms we enjoy exist because our forebears fought for them by refusing to accept the idea of TINA. They are the diamonds that our ancestors dug out from the dark pits of historical oppression to pass on to us today.

As we remember our debt to generations of activists before us, we need also to heed the words of the indigenous proverb: "We do not inherit the earth from our ancestors, we borrow it from our children."[14] The debts we have to those who came before and the duties to those who will come after constitute a moral imperative for every one of us to help out, however we can, in the various struggles for social justice.

But more than a duty, activism can also be a joy and a liberation. There is, perhaps, no way that we so fundamentally reject the notion of TINA as when we allow ourselves to hope that a better world is possible. And start to seek out others who agree.

Get involved!

Find out more at firedupbooks.ca.

NOTES

INTRODUCTION

1   Milton Friedman, *Capitalism and Freedom* (Chicago: University of Chicago Press, [1962] 2002).

2   Lawrence Mishel and Natalie Sabadish, "CEO Pay in 2012 Was Extraordinary High Relative to Typical Workers and Other High Earners," Economic Policy Institute 367 (June 2013).

3   Joel Bakan, *The Corporation* (Toronto: Penguin Canada, 2004), 49.

4   Unless otherwise specified dollar amounts are in U.S. dollars.

CHAPTER 1. THE MYTH OF TINA

1   The suicide rate averaged 12.1 per 100,000 people in the decade prior to the Depression, but jumped to an alarming 18.9 in 1929. In other words, there was an increase of 6.8 per 100,000. Given the population of the time (roughly 122 million), this works out to 8,296 additional suicides. See the U.S. Census, *Historical Statistics of the United States: Bicentennial Edition, Colonial Times to 1970*, vol. 1 (Washington, DC: 1975), 58.

2   Howard J. Sherman et al., *Economics: An Introduction to Traditional and Progressive Views*, 7th ed. (Armonk, NY: M.E. Sharpe, 2008), 158.

3   Western Europe's GDP: Dean Baker, Gerald Epstein, and Robert Pollin, eds., *Globalization and Progressive Economic Policy* (Cambridge: Cambridge University Press, 1998), 17. U.S. inequality: John Quiggin, *Zombie Economics: How Dead Ideas Still Walk among Us* (Princeton: Princeton University Press, 2010), 139. University enrolment: T.D. Snyder, ed., *120 Years of American Education: A Statistical Portrait*, vol. 1 (US Department of Education, 1993), 76–77.

4   Philip Armstrong, Andrew Glyn, and John Harrison, *Capitalism since 1945* (Oxford: Basil Blackwell, 1991), 229; Samuel Bowles, David M. Gordon, and Thomas E. Weisskopf, *After the Waste Land: A Democratic Economics for the Year 2000* (Armonk, NY: M. E. Sharpe, 1990).

5   David Harvey, *Brief History of Neoliberalism* (Oxford: Oxford University Press, 2005), 26.

6   Andrew Fieldhouse and Ethan Pollack, "Tenth Anniversary of the Bush-Era Tax Cuts," Economic Policy Institute 184 (2011).

7   Bowles, Gordon, and Weisskopf, *After the Waste Land*.

8   Phelps Brown quoted in Guy Standing, *Beyond the New Paternalism: Basic Security as Equality* (London: Verso, 2002), 56.

9   Robert Reich, *Saving Capitalism* (New York: Alfred A. Knopf, 2015), 116–17.

10 Joseph Stiglitz, *Globalization and Its Discontents* (London: Penguin, 2002).

11 Asad Ismi, "Impoverishing a Continent: The World Bank and the IMF in Africa" (Halifax: Halifax Initiative Coalition, 2004), 9.

12 Dan Kellar, "Presenting the Movement's Narratives," in *Whose Streets? The Toronto G20 and the Challenges of Summit Protest*, ed. Tom Malleson and David Wachsmuth (Toronto: Between the Lines, 2011), 73.

13 James P. Winter, *Lies the Media Tell Us* (Montreal: Black Rose, 2007).

14 Elections Canada, "The Electoral System of Canada," www.elections.ca.

15 Statistics in two paragraphs above: The Center for Responsive Politics, www.opensecrets.org.

16 Charles Lindblom, "The Market as Prison," *Journal of Politics* 44,2 (May 1982), 325.

1   E. Wolff, "Household Wealth Trends in the United States, 1962–2013: What Happened over the Great Recession?" *NBER Working Paper* 20733 (2014), 50.

2   This analogy is taken from David Schweickart, *After Capitalism*, 2nd ed. (Lanham, MD: Rowman & Littlefield, 2011), 90–94.

3   Deborah Hardoon, et al., "An Economy for the 1%," *Oxfam Briefing Paper* 210 (2016).

4   Richard Wilkinson and Kate Pickett, *The Spirit Level: Why Equality Is Better for Everyone* (London: Penguin Books, 2010).

5   Brian Barry, *Why Social Justice Matters* (Cambridge: Polity, 2005), 99–100.

6   Zoe Williams, "Don't Get Mad About the Mail's Use of the Philpotts to Tarnish the Poor—Get Even," *The Guardian*, www.theguardian.com, April 3, 2013.

7   Barry, *Why Social Justice Matters*, 47, 51.

8   Joan C. Tronto, *Caring Democracy: Markets, Equality, and Justice* (New York: New York University Press, 2013), 134; R. Scott Asen, "Is Private School Not Expensive Enough," *The New York Times,* www.nytimes.com, Aug. 24, 2012.

9   Barry, *Why Social Justice Matters*, 58.

10 Sam Pizzigati, "The 'Self-Made' Myth: Our Hallucinating Rich," Institute for Policy Studies, http://inequality.org, Sept. 23, 2012.

11 Raj Chetty et al., "Where Is the Land of Opportunity? The Geography of Intergenerational Mobility in the United States" (National Bureau of Economic Research, 2014).

12 Centers for Disease Control and Prevention, "How Did Cause of Death Contribute to Racial Differences in Life Expectancy in the United States?," Data Brief, www.cdc.gov, July 2013; Statistics Canada, "Life Expectancy," www.statcan.gc.ca, Nov. 2015.

13 Branko Milanovic, *The Haves and the Have-Nots* (New York: Basic Books, 2011), 118–20.

14 Ha-Joon Chang, *23 Things They Don't Tell You About Capitalism* (London: Allen Lane, 2010), 24; Jon C. Messenger, Sangheon Lee, and Deirdre McCann, *Working Time around the World: Trends in Working Hours, Laws, and Policies in a Global Comparative Perspective* (London: Routledge, 2007).

15 George Breitman, ed., *Malcolm X Speaks* (New York: Grove Weidenfeld, 1990), 26.

16 Gar Alperovitz and Lew Daly, *Unjust Deserts* (New York: New Press, 2008), 140.

17 Thad Williamson, "Realizing Property-Owning Democracy: A 20-Year Strategy to Create an Egalitarian Distribution of Assets in the United States," in *Property-Owning Democracy: Rawls and Beyond*, ed. Martin O'Neill and Thad Williamson (Chichester: Wiley-Blackwell, 2012), 226–27.

18 A.A. Alchian and H. Demsetz, "Production, Information Costs, and Economic Organization," *The American Economic Review* 62,5 (Dec. 1972), 777, 783.

19 CanadaWithoutPoverty, "New Ontario Premier Wants Action on Welfare & Housing," www.cwp-csp.ca, Feb. 1, 2013.

20 John Lindemann, "Always Low Prices and Always Low Wages: Why the NLRB Should Seek and Issue *Gissel* Bargaining Orders at Wal-Mart," *Guild Practitioner* 61,4 (2004).

21 Jeff Madrick, "Why Jack Welch Knows about Changing Numbers," *Harper's*, Oct. 12, 2012.

22 Alchian and Demsetz, "Production, Information Costs, and Economic Organization," 781–82.

23 In Canada, for example, the most common jobs for men are retail salesperson, then truck driver, then retail manager. For women, the most common jobs are retail salesperson, then administrative assistant, then nurse. Statistics Canada, "Portrait of Canada's Labour Force," www12.statcan.gc.ca.

24 Alice Hines, "Walmart Fined by Labor Department for Denying Workers Overtime Pay, Agrees to Pay $4.8 Million in Back Wages," *Huffington Post*, www.huffingtonpost.com, Feb. 5, 2012.

25 Tom Malleson, *After Occupy: Economic Democracy for the 21st Century* (New York, NY: Oxford University Press, 2014), chapter 3.

26 This example is from Michael Walzer, *Spheres of Justice* (New York: Basic Books, 1983), 295–303.

27 Robert Dahl, *A Preface to Economic Democracy* (Berkeley: University of California Press, 1985), 111.

28 Tania Branigan, "Tenth Apparent Suicide at Foxconn iPhone Factory in China," *The Guardian*, www.theguardian.com, May 27, 2010.

1 Marc R. Horney, "Project Pig Production Planner" (University of California Cooperative Extension); Erik Assadourian, "The Rise and Fall of Consumer Cultures," *State of the World* (2010).

2 Five planets: Assadourian, "The Rise and Fall of Consumer Cultures." Consumption stats: Juliet B. Schor, *Plenitude* (New York: Penguin Press, 2010), 25–26.

3 Schor, *Plenitude*, 29.

4 George W. Bush, "At O'Hare, President Says 'Get on Board,'" press release, http://georgewbush-whitehouse.archives.gov, Sept. 27, 2001; "President Holds Prime Time News Conference," press release, Oct. 11, 2001.

5 $140 billion on advertising: John Wolfe, "GroupM Forecasts 2012 Global Ad Spending to Increase 6.4%," WPP, www.wpp.com, Dec. 5, 2011. $135 billion on welfare: This is the sum of basic assistance (TANF), supplemental nutrition assistance program, school lunches, children's health insurance program, rental assistance, special supplemental nutrition program for woman, infants, and children, and low-income home energy assistance. Kevin Drum, "How Much Do We Spend on the Nonworking Poor?," *Mother Jones*, www.motherjones.com, Feb. 13, 2012. 90 percent: André Gorz, *Critique of Economic Reason* (London: Verso, 1989), 119. 630,000 ads: There is a wide range of estimates of how many ads the average American sees, from 200 to several thousand per day. I use a conservative estimate from *Consumer Reports*, which estimates 247 ads each day. See estimates at www.frankwbaker.com/adsinaday.htm. 93 percent: John de Graaf, David Wann, and Thomas H. Naylor, *Affluenza: The All-Consuming Epidemic*, 2nd ed. (San Francisco: Berrett-Koehle, 2005), 13.

6 Suzuki, cited in Catherine S. Hill and Margreta Morgulas, "Regional and State-Based Climate Change Initiatives in the United States," *Government, Law and Policy Journal* 10,1 (2008).

7 Aristotle, "Nicomachean Ethics," in *The Broadview Anthology of Social and Political Thought*, ed. Andrew Bailey et al. (Peterborough: Broadview, 2008).

8 Juliet B. Schor, *The Overworked American* (New York: Basic Books, 1991).

9 B. Russell, *In Praise of Idleness: And Other Essays* (London: G. Allen & Unwin, 1958).

10 Gerhard Bosch and Steffen Lehndorff, "Working-Time Reduction and Employment: Experiences in Europe and Economic Policy Recommendations," *Cambridge Journal of Economics* 25,2 (2001).

11 Richard Layard, *Happiness: Lessons from a New Science* (London: Allen Lane, 2005); Robert LaJeunesse, *Work Time Regulation as a Sustainable Full Employment Strategy: The Social Effort Bargain* (London: Routledge, 2009).

12 For instance, see Layard, *Happiness: Lessons from a New Science*; Daniel Kahneman et al., "A Survey Method for Characterizing Daily Life Experience: The Day Reconstruction Method," *Science* 306,5702 (2004).

13 LaJeunesse, *Work Time Regulation*, 84.

14 Philip Brickman, Dan Coates, and Ronnie Janoff-Bulman, "Lottery Winners and Accident Victims: Is Happiness Relative?," *Journal of Personality and Social Psychology* 36,8 (1978).

15 Matthew J. Slaughter, "Globalization and Declining Unionization in the United States," *Industrial Relations: A Journal of Economy and Society* 46,2 (April 2007).

16 Naomi Klein, *No Logo* (Toronto: Vintage Canada, 2000).

17 Jane Humphries, "Child Labor: Lessons from the Historical Experience of Today's Industrial Economies," *The World Bank Economic Review* 17,2 (Dec. 2003).

18 The AR5 uses the figures of 40%–70% reduction vis-à-vis the baseline of 2010. Total greenhouse gas emissions, however, are 31% higher in 2010 than the previous AR4 baseline of 1990. IPCC, "Climate Change 2014 Synthesis Report Summary for Policymakers," www.ipcc.ch, 20-22.

19 Ibid., 22.

20 These stats from George Monbiot, *Heat* (Toronto: Doubleday Canada, 2006); Bill McKibben, *Deep Economy* (New York: Times Books, 2007). See also T. Malleson, "A Community-Based Good Life or Eco-Apartheid," *Radical Philosophy Review* (2015).

21 R. Hilborn et al., "State of the World's Fisheries," *Annual Review of Environment and Resources* 28 (2003), 15.12.

22 Barry, *Why Social Justice Matters*, 253.

23 Assadourian, "The Rise and Fall of Consumer Cultures."

24 C.S. Maier, quoted in Donald Sassoon, *One Hundred Years of Socialism* (London: I.B. Tauris Publishers, 1996), 280.

25 Tom Jackson, *Prosperity without Growth: Economics for a Finite Planet* (London: Earthscan, 2005).

26 Boulding quoted in Schweickart, *After Capitalism*, 3.

CHAPTER 4. SHORT-TERM ALTERNATIVES

1 The top 1 percent of U.S. households has a mean income of $1,787,000. (E. Wolff, "Recent Trends in Household Wealth in the United States: Rising Debt and the Middle-Class Squeeze—an Update to 2007," The Levy Economics Institute Working Paper Collection 589 (2010), 46.) It has an average tax rate of 23.39 percent. (Richard Morrison, "The Tax Rate Paid by the Top 1% Is Double the National Average," Tax Foundation, http://taxfoundation.org, Nov. 30, 2012.) This leaves an average after-tax income of $1,369,000. So if we tax $369,000 of this to leave a million-dollar income, this provides revenue of $428 billion (multiplying 369,000 by the number of households in the 1 percent, which from Wolff p. 45 is 1,160,000).

The cost of the programs are $63 billion for free tuition (Jordan Weissmann, "Here's Exactly How Much the Government Would Have to Spend to Make Public College Tuition-Free," *The Atlantic*, www.theatlantic.com, Jan. 3, 2014);$22 billion for universal preschool (Cynthia G. Brown et al., "Investing in Our Children," Center for American Progress, www.americanprogress.org, Feb. 7, 2013); $176 billion to increase welfare rates (currently at $235 billion) by 75 percent (Drum, "How Much Do We Spend on the Nonworking Poor?"); $113 billion for maternity leave ("Universal Paid Maternity Leave in the US: What Would It Cost?," KellyMom, http://kellymom.com); and $60 billion for the Millennium Development Goals (Shantayanan Devarajan, Margaret J. Miller, and Eric V. Swanson, "The Costs of Attaining the Millennium Development Goals," The World Bank, www.worldbank.org/html/extdr/mdgassessment.pdf). This comes to a total of $434 billion.

2 Top tax rates: Quiggin, *Zombie Economics*. Reagan: Michel Albert, *Capitalism against Capitalism*, trans. Paul Haviland (London: Whurr Publishers, 1993), 1.

3 Union membership: Bowles, Gordon, and Weisskopf, *After the Waste Land*. Wage inequality: Michael Wallerstein, "Wage-Setting Institutions and Pay Inequality in Advanced Industrial Societies," in *Selected Works*

of *Michael Wallerstein: The Political Economy of Inequality, Unions, and Social Democracy*, ed. David Austen-Smith et al. (Cambridge: Cambridge University Press, 2008), 252.

4 Trond Randoy and Jim Nielsen, "Company Performance, Corporate Governance, and CEO Compensation in Norway and Sweden," *Journal of Management and Governance* 6 (2002); "The Rich, the Poor and the Growing Gap between Them," *The Economist*, June 15, 2006.

5 Jonas Pontusson, *Inequality and Prosperity: Social Europe vs. Liberal America* (Ithaca: Cornell University Press, 2005).

6 The U.S. figure is from 2013 in order to be consistent with earlier in the chapter. The Swedish figure, from 2013 as well, comes from "Trade Unions," worker-participation.eu.

7 OECD, Revenue Statistics 2015 (Paris: OECD Publishing, 2015), 80.

8 "Warren Buffett and His Secretary on Their Tax Rates," ABC News, http://abcnews.go.com, Jan. 25, 2012.

9 Aditya Chakrabortty, "I've Found the Key to Britain's Recovery: An Orange Shed in Shanktown," *The Guardian*, www.theguardian.com, March 29, 2016.

10 George Monbiot, "A Telling Silence," www.monbiot.com, Jan. 21, 2013.

11 Pontusson, *Inequality and Prosperity*, 134.

12 "Once Again a Model: Nordic Social Democracy in a Globalized World," in *What's Left of the Left: Democrats and Social Democrats in Challenging Times*, ed. James Cronin, George Ross, and James Shoch (Durham: Duke University Press, 2011), 97.

13 Jody Heymann, Alison Earle, Jeffrey Hayes, "The Work, Family, and Equity Index: How Does the United States Measure Up?" (Montreal and Boston: Project on Global Working Families, McGill Institute for Health and Social Policy, 2007), www.mcgill.ca/ihsp.

14 Karen Sternheimer, *Everyday Sociology Reader* (New York: W. W. Norton & Company, 2010), 254–56.

15 Gregory Dow, *Governing the Firm: Workers' Control in Theory and Practice* (Cambridge: Cambridge University Press, 2003).

16 Doug Pyper and Feargal McGuinness, "Zero-Hours Contracts," House of Commons Library, Briefing Paper 06553, www.parliament.uk, Feb. 25, 2015.

17 LaJeunesse, *Work Time Regulation*.

18 Robert Skidelsky and Edward Skidelsky, *How Much Is Enough? Money and the Good Life* (New York: Other Press, 2012).

19 J.M. Keynes, "National Self-Sufficiency," *The Yale Review* 22,4 (1933), 181.

20 Ray Hilborn, J.M. Lobo Orensanz, and Ana M. Parma, "Institutions, Incentives and the Future of Fisheries," *Philosophical Transactions of the Royal Society B: Biological Sciences* 360,1453 (Jan. 29, 2005).

21 P.L. Joskow, R. Schmalensee, and E.M. Bailey, "The Market for Sulfur Dioxide Emissions," *American Economic Review* 88,4 (Sept. 1998); D. Malakoff, "Taking the Sting out of Acid Rain," *Science* 330,6006 (Nov. 12, 2010).

22 UNDP, *Human Development Report 2007/2008* (Houndmills: Palgrave Macmillan, 2007), 41.

23 See the video debate at www.munkdebates.com/debates/taxing-the-rich.

24 These stats refer to the inequality-adjusted measure of the Human Development Index, UNDP, "Human Development Report 2013," http://hdr.undp.org.

25 Julia B. Isaacs, "International Comparisons of Economic Mobility," *Getting Ahead or Losing Ground: Economic Mobility in America*, ed. Ron Haskins, Julia B. Isaacs, and Isabel V. Sawhill (Washington, DC: Economic Mobility Project, Pew Charitable Trusts, 2008).

26 Richard Wilkinson, "How Economic Inequality Harms Society," Ted Talks, www.ted.com/talks/richard_wilkinson.html.

27 This is a paraphrase of a famous expression from R.H. Tawney, *Equality* (London: George Allen & Unwin Ltd, 1931), 164.

28 Nicholas D. Kristof, "The Wrong Side of History," *The New York Times*, www.nytimes.com, Nov. 11, 2009; Paul Krugman, "Insurance and Freedom," *The New York Times*, www.nytimes.com, April 8, 2013.

29 Paul Hirst, *Associative Democracy* (Cambridge: Polity Press, 1994).

30 GDP per capita is measured in purchasing-power parity. Data for this and growth rates are from Pontusson, *Inequality and Prosperity*, 5. For employment data see Paul Krugman, "Multidimensional Europe," *The New York Times*, http://krugman.blogs.nytimes.com, Jan. 1, 2011.

31 Arthur Nelson, "Wind Power Generates 140% of Denmark's Electricity Demand," *The Guardian*, www.theguardian.com, July 10, 2015.

1 G.D.H. Cole, *Guild Socialism Re-stated* (London: Leonard Parsons, 1920), 20.

2 Robert Dahl, *On Democracy* (New Haven: Yale University Press, 2000), 71.

3 Important works on Mondragon include William Foote Whyte and Kathleen King Whyte, *Making Mondragon: The Growth and Dynamics of the Worker Cooperative Complex* (Ithaca, NY: ILR Press, 1988); Roy Morrison, *We Build the Road as We Travel* (Warner, NH: Essential Book Publishers, 1997); S. Arando et al., "Assessing Mondragon: Stability and Managed Change in the Face of Globalization," William Davidson Institute Working Paper no. 1003 (2010).

4 John Restakis, *Humanizing the Economy: Co-operatives in the Age of Capital* (Gabriola Island: New Society Publishers, 2010).

5 Dow, *Governing the Firm*; Malleson, *After Occupy*.

6 K.V. Berman, *Worker-Owned Plywood Companies: An Economic Analysis* (Pullman, WA: Washington State University Press, 1967); Ben Craig and John Pencavel, "Participation and Productivity: A Comparison of Worker Cooperatives and Conventional Firms in the Plywood Industry," Brookings Papers on Economic Activity: Microeconomics 1995 (1995); J.R. Cable and F.R. FitzRoy, "Productive Efficiency, Incentives and Employee Participation: Some Preliminary Results for West Germany," *Kyklos* 33,1 (Feb. 1980); W. Bartlett et al., "Labor-Managed Cooperatives and Private Firms in North Central Italy: An Empirical Comparison," *Industrial and Labor Relations Review* 46,1 (Oct. 1992); Ornella Wanda Maietta and Vania Sena, "Is Competition Really Bad News for Cooperatives? Some Empirical Evidence for Italian Producers' Cooperatives," *Journal of Productivity Analysis* 29,3 (June 2008); Alberto Zevi, "The Performance of Italian Producer Cooperatives," in *Participatory and Self-Managed Firms*, ed. Derek Jones and Jan Svenjar (Lexington, MA: LexingtonBooks, 1982); Bodil Thordarson, "A Comparison of Worker-Owned Firms and Conventionally Owned Firms in Sweden," *Advances in the Economics of Participatory and Self-Managed Firms* 2 (1987); Niels Mygind, "Are Self-Managed Firms Efficient? The Experience of Danish Fully and Partly Self-Managed Firms," *Advances in the Economics of Participatory and Labor-Managed Firms* 2 (1987); J.S. Defourny, "Comparative Measures of Technical Efficiency for Five

Hundred French Workers' Cooperatives," ibid., 4 (1992); Fathi Fakhfakh, Virginie Perotin, and Monica Gago, "Productivity, Capital and Labor in Labor-Managed and Conventional Firms," *TEPP Working Paper* 2011-8 (2009); José Alberto Bayo-Moriones, Pedro Javier Galilea-Salvatierra, and Javier Merino-Díaz De Cerio, "Participation, Cooperatives and Performance: An Analysis of Spanish Manufacturing Firms," *Advances in the Economic Analysis of Participatory and Labor-Managed Firms* 7 (2003); Henk Thomas and Chris Logan, *Mondragon: An Economic Analysis* (London: G. Allen & Unwin, 1982).

7 Edward S. Greenberg, *Workplace Democracy: The Political Effects of Participation* (Ithaca, NY: Cornell University Press, 1986), 44.

8 Dow, *Governing the Firm*, 227.

9 For evidence on wages in co-ops see ibid. For wage inequality in social democratic countries see, Randoy and Nielsen, "Company Performance, Corporate Governance, and CEO Compensation in Norway and Sweden." For the U.S., see Mishel and Sabadish, "CEO Pay in 2012." J.C. Bogle, "Reflections on CEO Compensation," *The Academy of Management Perspectives* [formerly *The Academy of Management Executive*] *(AMP)* 22,2 (2008).

10 Philippe Van Parijs, "A Basic Income for All," *Boston Review* 25,5 (Feb./March 2000). For an academic, philosophical argument see Van Parijs, *Real Freedom for All* (Oxford: Clarendon Press, 1995).

11 Karen McVeigh, "US Emergency Food Providers Brace as $5bn Food Stamp Cuts Set In," *The Guardian*, www.theguardian.com, Nov. 1, 2013.

12 It is difficult to calculate exactly how much a UBI would cost because the taxes needed would depend on how people react to its implementation. The more that people go part-time or quit work altogether, the higher taxes would have to go. On the other hand, there would be some savings from the fact that the UBI could potentially replace a number of existing programs.

13 Herbert A. Simon, "Public Administration in Today's World of Organizations and Markets," *PS: Political Science and Politics* 33,4 (Dec. 2000), 755–56.

14 The median adult income in the United States in 2013 was $27,851 (U.S. Census Bureau, "Pinc-01. Selected Characteristics of People 15 Years Old and Over by Total Money Income in 2013," www.census.gov). To get the disposable income, we divide this figure by the effective tax rate, which for this income was roughly 22.5 percent (Citizens for Tax

Justice, "Who Pays Taxes in America in 2013?," http://ctj.org, April 1, 2013). This gives us a rough estimate for median personal disposable income of $21,585.

In 2013, average labour productivity in the United States was $66 per worker per hour (OECD, "Level of GDP Per Capita and Productivity: Level of GDP per Capita and Productivity—Most Recent Year," http://stats.oecd.org). The current U.S. public sector is funded through taxation representing 25 percent of GDP, whereas one of the world's most generous public system is Sweden's at 45 percent. This high level of taxation allows for universal daycare, free primary and secondary education, free university, an excellent system of public health care, good pensions, extensive public transport, sixteen months of parental leave, generous welfare and disability benefits, retraining programs for workers to find new work, etc. So let us assume that a socialist society funds its public sector at the rate of 55 percent of GDP. This represents a 10 percent improvement over Sweden's level of service provision, more than double current U.S. spending on social services, and enough to fund Swedish-style services and a UBI. If for the sake of simplicity we assume that all taxation comes in the form of income tax, then each worker would require an income of $48,000 pre-tax to end up with the basic amount of $21,600 post-tax. At prevailing rates of productivity, this income requires an average of only 727 hours of work, i.e., 15 hours of work per week or 3.0 hours per day (assuming four weeks holiday and the same percentage of population in the labour force as currently).

15 Erik Olin Wright, *Envisioning Real Utopias* (London: Verso, 2010).

16 Brian Wampler, *Participatory Budgeting in Brazil* (University Park, PA: Pennsylvania State University Press, 2007); Gregory Wilpert, *Changing Venezuela by Taking Power* (London: Verso, 2007).

17 The following description is based on ideas from a number of socialists, particularly Schweickart, *After Capitalism*.

18 John Rawls, *A Theory of Justice* (Cambridge, MA: Harvard University Press, 1971), 102.

CHAPTER 6. SOMETHING TO FIGHT FOR

1 For a heart-wrenching account of life in England in early 1900s, see Robert Tressell, *The Ragged Trousered Philanthropists* (London: Penguin, [1914] 2004).

2 Quoted in Martin Luther King, *I Have a Dream: Writings and Speeches That Changed the World*, ed. James M. Washington (New York: Harper-One, 1992), 75.

3 Simon Rogers, "Occupy Protests around the World: Full List Visualized," *The Guardian,* www.theguardian.com, Oct. 17, 2011.

4 Rudolf Meidner, *Employee Investment Funds: An Approach to Collective Capital Formation* (London: G. Allen & Unwin, 1978).

5 Jonas Pontusson, *The Limits of Social Democracy: Investment Politics in Sweden* (New York: Cornell University Press, 1992).

6 Malleson, *After Occupy.*

7 Robert Graham, ed., *Anarchism: A Documentary History of Libertarian Ideas,* vol. 1 (Montreal: Black Rose, 2005), 490.

8 Howard Zinn, *A People's History of the United States,* 2nd ed. (New York: Longman, 1996).

9 John Holloway, *Change the World without Taking Power* (London: Pluto Press, 2002).

10 Robin Hahnel, "Venezuela: Not What You Think," Znet, www.zcommunications.org.

11 Vladimir Ilyich Lenin, "What Is to Be Done?," Marxists.org.

12 "The history of all countries shows that the working class, exclusively by its own effort, is able to develop only trade union consciousness." Ibid. Lenin was very critical of the idea of workplace democracy: "a producer's congress! What precisely does that mean? It is difficult to find words to describe this folly. I keep asking myself can they be joking? Can one really take these people seriously? While production is always necessary, democracy is not. Democracy of production engenders a series of radically false ideas." Quoted in Michael Albert and Robin Hahnel, *Looking Forward: Participatory Economics for the 21st Century* (Boston: South End, 1991), 22.

13 For careful historical examination of how Lenin's vanguard (and his top-down political structures more generally) did *not* wither away but in fact grew naturally into Stalin's dictatorship, see Maurice Brinton, *The Bolsheviks & Workers' Control, 1917–1921* (Black Rose, 1975).

14 The precise origins of this phrase are unknown. It is sometimes attributed to the Duwamish leader Chief Seattle, and sometimes to the environmentalist Wendell Berry.

INDEX

Shelfie

An **ebook** edition is available for $2.99
with the purchase of this print book.

ISBN 978-1-77113-200-8